Soul Sabbatical

How to Regain Your Time, Joy, and Energy

Yolanda Harper

Printed in the United States of America

First Printing, 2023

ISBN (print) 979-8-218-28518-0

ISBN (ebook) 979-8-218-28519-7

For more information, visit: https://yolandaharper.com/

Contents

Praise for "Soul Sabbatical"

When Yolanda took her sabbatical, I watched and listened with awe and wonder. I was so curious - how on earth could she do that and her business not totally implode? She did do it and the business did not, in fact, implode. Moreover, she became brighter and more connected to what truly matters. It inspired me to wonder if I could also pull something like that off. I managed to follow in her footsteps in my own way. My business didn't implode, either.

Yolanda's journey that inspired me to live life differently is gift-wrapped in these pages for you. It's a balm to a hustle-weary heart and a beckoning to enter a better reality that seems like a dream. Yolanda is a truly capable doula helping you usher your soul sabbatical into this world.

– Tabitha Westbrook, licensed therapist, author, speaker

Soul Sabbatical is a transformative exploration of how to let go of Hustle You and reconnect your heart with your head and soul. Many of us know busyness, overfunctioning, and the pressure to do things right isn't working, but we have no idea how to fix it. Yolanda welcomes the reader to follow her healing journey with openness, curiosity, and a spirit of embracing the unknown. Her experience inspires others to not only change the things they are doing but also change the approach they take to living an easeful and fulfilling life. *Soul Sabbatical* is an invaluable resource for those seeking a deeper understanding of their inner world and forging a path to reviving their heart.

– Erika Labuzan-Lopez, LMFT-S, LPC-S

In *Soul Sabbatical* by Yolanda, reading transcends its conventional bounds; it becomes an immersive journey. Today, as we grapple with an insatiable longing for a kind of rest that sleep alone cannot provide, Yolanda's innovative concept of taking a 'soul sabbatical' emerges as a profound answer to the pervasive soul weariness we endure.

The book creates an exquisite tension within as you embark on this transformative voyage. To reach the coveted haven of rest, one must bravely shed preconceived notions and dare to release the tightly held constructs of success that we've toiled so diligently to attain.

It has been an extraordinary privilege to contribute to the realization of this remarkable book. Yolanda, I extend my heartfelt gratitude for sharing your wisdom with the world.

– Jo Muirhead, Carer Loving Mum, Founder & Director - Purple Co.

Soul Sabbatical is a beautiful invitation to live, open-hearted, centered, and grounded in a way like you never have before. Yolanda has walked this walk and through her vulnerability, speaks to your heart in a way that compels you to quit the late-stage capitalism game and honor yourself. Radical and counter-cultural, the prompts will guide you towards a more whole you. What a rich, deep life there is up ahead! Thank you Yolanda for writing a book that is a drop of healing that will ripple out into the world for generations to come.

– Kelly Higdon, MFT, Reiki Master, Author, Speaker, Consultant

Yolanda Harper had proven herself a remarkably effective therapist when I was a Circuit Court Judge handling children and adults with histories of adversity and trauma.

As an author, she takes one down a path that leads to a better understanding of oneself and of healing. Your heart will delight as you discover ways that we each can experience and leave a "love legacy" of healing, love of self, and kindness. Her printed words invite your heart to travel with her on a *Soul Sabbatical*.

– *Lynn Tepper, Retired Florida Circuit Court Judge*

As I looked at the title of this book, I thought the idea of a soul sabbatical sounded luxurious, perhaps not realistic, but I was curious. As I dove into the story of Yolanda Harper and her journey, I saw so much of myself, right down to the temper tantrum. I resonated with the cycle of overwhelm and burnout, coming up for air and sorting through, only to find myself in the cycle again. I nodded, felt seen, and challenged by the societal barriers resulting in some of my mindset barriers.

Yolanda's blend of her own story, knowledge, and growth kept me incredibly engaged, and before I knew it, I was at the end. It was only at the end that I realized the richness and density of the content. I found myself processing what I had read over several days, recognizing that a soul sabbatical is not an event but a practice. As a mental health professional, I recognize the consequences of not listening to our soul are dissatisfaction, burnout, anxiety, and depression, just to name a few. Yolanda invites us to align by listening to the conflict of what is driving us and where our soul desires to be and become by outlining a practice we all can use. Thank you, Yolanda, for sharing your story, knowledge, and insight so we too can have our own soul sabbatical. I am inviting my heart.

– *Cyndi Doyle, LPC-S, NCC, CDWF, Code4Couples.com*

To weary hearts everywhere:

Welcome Home.

Dear Hustle You,

Thank you for all you have done. You learned to survive in a dangerous world. One that pays no respect to what happens below the neck. One that makes you have to armor your heart and soul. Your hustle has gained success. Respect. Influence. A rich life, full of every material item you could ever want or need. You have respect. Fortune.

You did what you saw all around you. What you've been taught. I honor and appreciate that.

But it's come at a cost...To your health. To your relationships. To your heart and your soul.

The hustle has cost you peace. Joy. Connection with yourself and others. The hustle is heavy – like a two ton piece of armor that you carry around all of the time.

Preface

The hustle has cut off oxygen and blood supply to me, your heart. It's caused me to wither.

But it's time for things to be different now.

It's time to breathe love, light, and life back into me so that you can truly live because you realize that you can no longer go on only half living. And that means that you'll slow down.   And start to pay attention to me again.

Because you remember that I've been here all along.

And it's time to reconnect.

With love,
Your reviving heart

Foreword
Rebekah Gregory

I remember the first phone call I received when Yolanda told me she had decided to write a book. Her voice trembled with nervous excitement, and I could almost sense her shaky hands through the phone. My immediate reaction was to ecstatically scream and jump for joy, shouting, "FINALLY!" To know Yolanda is to love her, and even before reading a single chapter, I knew her words would reveal her brilliance to the world. Then, my immediate question was, why did she seem so hesitant? Didn't she realize how profoundly this book would impact lives? But that's what makes her truly remarkable.

You see, there are two kinds of people in this world. There are those who project an image of having it all together, making you feel the immense pressure to live up to their carefully curated highlight reel. And then there are those like Yolanda, who are willing to expose the most vulnerable parts of themselves in the most loving way, providing a soft place to land for others when life isn't picture perfect.

I believe this is where our world is still lacking and why this book is so necessary. We are more connected than ever, but often it's to anything other than ourselves and the people around us. Why? Because sifting through the challenges that life throws our way can be terrifying. It becomes much easier for us to put on a facade, apply a pretty filter, and pretend that everything is okay. The things we do for "the gram," right?

After surviving the Boston Marathon bombing in 2013, my own facade crumbled. I quickly learned that if I had any chance of navigating the darkest days I had ever faced, I could no longer put myself on the back burner or avoid confronting my own obstacles. I had to face them head-on. Over the past decade, that's precisely what I've attempted to do—through 76 exhausting surgeries, the loss of my left leg below the knee, testifying in the trial of the remaining bomber, and confronting childhood trauma, among other trials. But none of this was done alone, nor could it have been. And while my body may appear battered and broken, I am more healthy and whole than I have ever been, thanks to people like Yolanda. People who possess the tools, knowledge, and compassion to show me what it means to live life to the fullest rather than merely surviving it.

For several years now, I have had the immense privilege of witnessing families heal and hearts mend because of Yolanda Harper. I have also experienced the light she has brought into my own ongoing recovery journey. I met Yolanda shortly after my family moved to Florida in 2018. We had founded a nonprofit called Rebekah's Angels to provide mental health therapy to children and families. Yolanda came to us as a therapist referral and quickly became one of my dearest friends. As you read these pages, you will understand why it's effortless for me to write this foreword for her. The person you will encounter in these chapters is not only one of the finest in her field but also one of the most exceptional human beings I've ever had the pleasure of knowing.

Foreword

Without a doubt, every ounce of her heart and soul has gone into making this book spectacular, and it is indeed spectacular. However, it's not just the letters behind her name that grant her the credentials and authority to write something like this; it's the "why" behind it. You will discover that it was Yolanda's own trauma and suffering that drove her to become a therapist, and I believe that speaks volumes. She "gets it," not simply because she took college classes to become certified (although she certainly did), but because she has lived through the pain, the hopelessness, the worry, the anger, the imposter syndrome, and the triumph herself. Today, while she most certainly shines from her mountaintop, she also exposes her valleys like never before. Why? Because she wants you to reach your mountaintop too. She wants to offer you the comfort that connecting with your soul can provide, and she knows that she has accumulated what it takes to guide you there.

But "Soul Sabbatical" isn't just a book that you purchase and leave on your coffee table or bookshelf. It is instead one that you'll highlight, earmark, take notes on, and remember long after you've finished reading it. "Soul Sabbatical" is a transformation, something that everyone needs to experience repeatedly. It's about the vulnerability of putting in the hard work to understand our true selves so that we can live our lives doing what we love, instead of letting unnecessary stressors steal our precious time.

I feel incredibly fortunate to call Yolanda my friend. I am immensely proud of her for finally writing this book, and I'm thrilled for you to read it and become just as captivated as I am as you embark on your own "Soul Sabbatical."

–*Rebekah Gregory, Founder of Rebekah's Angels Foundation, Speaker, Author*

Introduction

Introduction

Hi, I'm Yolanda

I'm a business owner, trauma therapist, researcher, TEDx Speaker, trainer, and mentor....

"Hustle Me" wanted to make sure you know these things from the get-go.

I'm also a wife, human mom, dog mom, and friend. I am a daughter and sister who grew up in a very chaotic, often emotionally, verbally, and physically abusive home.

And this is the first time I've expressed this fact in such a public format.

Because if you're a similar high-functioning, pull yourself up by your bootstraps, getting shit done, I WILL handle anything life throws at me, high performing...

- Exhausted
- Resentful
- There's never a quiet moment
- I'm barely keeping my head above water but somehow got people fooled that I have my shit together, person....

Then I can almost guarantee you've had your fair share of life wounds, too.

Your trauma might have looked like this:

- Walking on eggshells
- Learning that you needed to stay small and invisible to stay safe
- Not having anyone to protect you
- Having to be the adult in kid's clothing
- Abuse

Introduction

- An addicted caregiver
- Chronically being taken advantage of by people who should have known better.

You work hard to be perfect and keep everything within the rails.

You are a workaholic.

You skirt right along the edge of "too much" of the things that are socially acceptable – drinking, shopping, sexing, or numbing too much before you reign it back under control... until the next time.

You work out. A little too hard. Or you cut or binge and purge.

You stopped listening to your heart and soul, your wants and needs, a long time ago... that is, if you ever realized you could listen to them at all.

When you were younger, you could double down on all of these.

But, as you get older and older, it's harder and harder to do (and you kind of don't want to anymore, if you're honest with yourself).

Abusing yourself to hustle in hopes of discovering your value and worth is taking a toll on your relationships (when will "enough" ever be enough?), your body, mind, and heart.

ESPECIALLY your heart. You've locked it away for so long to protect it, but it's calling you. And the call is getting louder and more urgent.

And here, in this space, your heart is invited to beat again.

You are invited to get to know yourself. The part of you that's been buried under the rubble and is ready to come to life.

Introduction

That burning sense that there must be more to life than this... yes.

That pressing sense that time is running out to make the changes you need to get there... yes.

I've seen it not only in the women I work with. I've faced it head-on in myself.

Life taught me early on to disconnect from myself, to abandon the subtle cries from my soul.

I mean, who was I to have wants? Who was I to have needs? Who was I to dream?

Who was I to matter enough to challenge the status quo?

Who was I to believe that I deserved something... more.

This book is a personal reflection of me returning to my heart, recognizing my dreams, claiming my desires, and in the process, learning what it means to truly love myself and allow myself to truly be loved. I learned how to rest, play, and connect deeply to myself and those I care about.

This is the practice of a *Soul Sabbatical*.

I want to share how you can do this, too.

How can you identify the things keeping you from the joy, peace, and connection your heart desires? To find the roadmap to your heart and a sense of balance and fulfillment in your life. And to create daily, easeful practices that help you redefine success in your life with a sense of newness and abundance.

My *Soul Sabbatical* is an event and is becoming my way of life. It will remain an ongoing practice for me in the remaining years of my life.

Introduction

I hope it will be for you as well.

May YOU know your worth.
May YOU trust your wisdom.
May YOU be a force to be reckoned with.
May YOU love and be loved.

Part One

Head Check

Chapter 1
The Great Resignation

As a therapist, I'm known for doing the "deep work." I want to take clients beyond first-order change, where we change a behavior only to have another pop up in its place like a game of whack-a-mole. When we can take a look deeper into the root cause of what led to the place we're at now, the changes that can be made are longer-lasting and more meaningful.

This deep work requires us to make the implicit explicit. To name the things that don't get named. To wrap words around the truth of our experiences.

It took me forever to name that I was burned out. I struggled to admit to myself that I wanted more out of life than the status quo. Because I live a pretty blessed life, I had a hard time acknowledging that I yearned for more joy, peace, and connection. For a greater sense of simplicity, balance, and ease.

So many of us go through this kind of half-living. Things are "good enough" for us to grit our teeth, grin, and bear it. But our souls long for more.

So, ok. These are the things I wanted to change. But how did I get to the space that this is what needed to change? What had been happening to set the current state in stone? I started to dig in there.

And in that excavation, I started to put words around behaviors and systems that led to where I was. Ingrained habits like perfectionism, comparison, over-helping, people pleasing, performing, and over-functioning. As I started digging beneath these behaviors into what fuels them, I started making connections to massive systems of hyper-capitalism and patriarchy (plus the racism, ageism, heterosexism, and other - isms that result from these systems).

To be clear, there's no quick and easy fix to these broken systems, but we can take a closer look at some of the ways that they impact each of us and gain some agency in how we can respond.

To not do so further enslaves us to these systems. And further strengthens them. Maybe we can't completely topple them, but we can start putting cracks in their foundations. Looking deeper helps us to find our voice and use it. To recognize the things that are harming us. It helps us to take fierce action – like the Great Resignation.

There's a trend happening across the country of people leaving their jobs. The latest numbers are that 4.5 million people resigned in November 2021 alone!

I QUIT TOO.

Ok, technically, I got a new job description (more about my Chief Vision Officer role to come), but my sabbatical gave me some time and space to explore and practice quitting a lot of things that don't work for me...

And by "practice," I mean wrestle with, rage against, and try on different ways that feel super foreign and uncomfortable. But at this point, the wisest parts of me are insisting that we can't go on in the same way, and I'm doing my best to listen.

(And listening is the most important part. I've taught myself, proven to my heart time and time again, that I'm listening. That I'm worth the time, space, and energy of listening.)

The Things I Quit:

Overfunctioning. When things get tough (hello, seeing clients and trying to run a business and take care of my family during a pandemic and upheaval after upheaval– the past years have basically been one opportunity after the next to overfunction), my pattern for dealing with the uncertainty and chaos is to spin into super drive because ohmygodit'ssohardjustfixitalready, but in reality it's me adding one more thing to do and exhausting myself. And, in case you're wondering, I am NOT a delight to be around when I'm exhausted.

Think of over-functioning as the PIVOT on steroids. I know something needs to change, but I don't yet know what it is or how to change it, so I throw the whole pot of spaghetti noodles on the wall to see what sticks, but don't actually wait to see what's working before I boil a whole other pot of noodles and start slinging them too. (If this feels like a long sentence, then you're getting a sense of what over-functioning FEELS like). By the way, I'm not a good cook, either. My noodles never stick right.

Performing. I want to be the "good wife/mother/friend/professional" and can try to force myself into society's mold of what this looks like so that people will "like" me. I try to tap dance, Electric Slide, or line dance, depending on what the people around me are doing, even though I can't dance at all. Blending in and making other people happy can be second nature to me (see also, Patriarchy below). Only, playing a role is exhausting, and, as mentioned above, I am NOT a delight to be around when I'm exhausted. (Hmm... I'm noticing a pattern here).

Comparison. UGH. This one sucks all the way around. Comparing always makes me feel like not only am I not doing enough, but there's no way to ever catch up. I see the people around me and want to do what they're doing, only better. This makes me put so much (unnecessary) pressure on myself and ends up making me shrink and feel constricted, in my mind and in my body. Comparison and performing go hand in hand for me. And, because I actually value community and collaboration, comparison makes me move outside of my values and integrity. Also exhausting and a little icky.

Capitalism. Actually, let's call it hyper-capitalism (because I actually think that good things can come from ethical capitalism that prioritizes not destroying people and the planet to make a profit). For the first time in my life, I'm holding some of these concepts at arm's length – especially the idea that my value and worth are tied to my "productivity"/income/money brought in. I'm realizing more and more how ingrained and toxic this is for me. I'm also learning how hard it is to unlearn.

When I'm in a place of basing my worth on my productivity, and I combine that with the scarcity of comparison, it's like lighting a Molotov cocktail - meltdown is going to quickly ensue. There will never be enough time to make enough money in the eyes of hyper-capitalism. Then, add the belief that one, if I don't get it, then you're getting it, and two, you're taking it away from me, and three, I need all of that money and then some. Whew.

Patriarchy. I'm quitting swallowing the poisonous patriarchal ways of not owning my truth and holding space for what my heart, soul, and being are crying out for. I quit the system that keeps me swimming in the shame of simultaneously being "not enough" and "too much." Patriarchy is such a complex, all-encompassing system that's so ingrained in us that it's hard to recognize the ways it's infiltrated so much of who we are, what we do, and the way we do it. But you can feel it. The injustice. The abuse of power-over. The dismissal. The box seats. The C-Suite. The fact that women are still arm candy and not in charge. The exploitation. I quit pretending that it's not there.

And, while we're at it, let's name other deadly systems of racism. Heterosexism. All of the -isms that cause us to have to shrink and hide and guard our hearts for our own survival. Thank God there's finally starting to be some reckoning in these spaces. These things, too, I quit pretending that I'm not an "other" in some of these spaces. It doesn't undo the damage that still is happening, but I know I'm not alone, where before, I was doing my best to fit in. Each one of us deserves to belong.

A combination of all of the above leads to me doing all of the things and being resentful, pissed off, completely exhausted, and hating myself for the way I show up in the world.

So I said "enough" and spent time during sabbatical getting an idea of what it would look like to quit each of these things. But, unlike the Great Resignation, I'm finding that I have to quit them time and time again. Almost on a daily basis– because I'm undoing years of stuff that's been ingrained. And quitting feels so good.

If you're like me, you're not a "quitter." If you're like me, you didn't know that you were "allowed" to quit. But the Great Resignation has shown me that, yes, indeed, it is possible to quit something that isn't, in fact, working for you.

Maybe the thought has tickled your mind and quickened your heart. We do get a choice to quit. Think with your mind, but even more, take a breath deep into your heart. What is the first thing you'd like to resign from, if you could choose something?

Sometimes, the things that I need to quit in order to hear my heart are clear to me. I see them with 20/20 vision and no smears on my glasses.

Other times, I'm blindsided. It's like a defensive lineman comes up from behind and takes me out at the knees – the next thing I know, I'm face-down on the turf.

That's what happened the other day when I said to my team,

8

"So and so asked me to do this."

Team:

"You don't have time to do that. What are you going to do, get up at 3 am to do it?"

Me:

Sure, I can do that.

Then, also Me:

Shit, they're right. "Ok, I hear you."

Hustle me would have said, "Screw you, you're not the boss of me!" Hustle me would have doubled down and not only done that thing but added ten more to the list, just for good measure.

Wiser me is trying to meet these moments with some fierce compassion and a little curiosity…

Why am I doing what I'm doing??

I got still with myself.

"Self, what's going on here??"

My heart started sharing its truth. With wisdom.

Now I'm adding these things to the list of things that I'm quitting:

People Pleasing. I want to be liked. I mean really, Really, REALLY liked. When people think of me, I want them to have an ethereal experience. I want the clouds to part, rays of sun to shine down, and the angels to sing. You know, no big deal.

Wise me to hustle me: "You know this is completely unrealistic, right?"

Hustle me: "Maybe this time will be different?? I mean, I'm pretty sure I heard the angels warming up."

Sigh. (Hustle me is nothing if not persistent. Or stubborn.)

Trying to live outside of the time/space continuum. I want to be able to have all of the time to be able to do all of the things without the restrictions of a 24-hour day or the needs of a human body to sleep, eat, and poop.

Hustle me: "Sleep? We don't need sleep! Who needs sleep?."

All the other parts of me raise their hands. "We do. We definitely need sleep."

Actually, it's not the wanting to help part that's the problem. Helping is what I do. It's ingrained in my DNA. The world needs helpers and our healing hearts, especially now. It's the "helping at all costs" that smothers my heart. Even though helping is second nature to me, doing the work that I do can come at a cost – mentally, emotionally, and especially spiritually. Unless I acknowledge that, take it into consideration, and take consistent and meaningful action to prevent it, I'll always be pouring from an empty cup. (My fellow helpers + healers, I know you know what I mean! We have to matter to ourselves in the work that we do.)

PS. There's also a strong patriarchal bent here that ingrains a sense that women take care of others without regard for their own needs.

I'm adding these to my quitting list now. I'm sure there are still several others that will be uncovered.

And because of the work that I do, I know that I'm not alone in having conversations with myself. I know that you do, too. And now, your heart is invited to the conversation.

Soul Sabbatical

Dear Perfectionism,
(A Note from My Heart)

You've been a constant companion for so long. I remember you from elementary school years. We weren't formally introduced, but I soon became well acquainted with what it felt like when you were around...

"Why did you get an A- and not an A+?"

And later...

"You can't say that."

"You can't go out looking like that."

"You can't be seen doing that."

Sound perfect.

Look perfect.

Be perfect.

Over time, our relationship deepened. One of survival. You taught me to beat others to the punch.

Be perfect, and others won't criticize you.

Be perfect, and you might find a place to belong.

Be perfect so that you will be loved.

Perfect is safe.

Like the perfect(ion) shield will keep me from ever feeling shame.

Only not.

Now I'm learning that perfectionism is a really heavy load to bear. Carrying you around used to feel like it made me safer, but now it feels so very exhausting.

I can't keep up with you and your constant, never-ending demands. And just when I feel like I'm getting close to meeting your totally unrealistic expectations, you move the bar. Over and over again. I feel like I'm constantly scrambling to keep up.

(By the way, haven't I seen you hanging around with the Patriarchy, getting all bossy about how "good girls" should be??)

I can't do it anymore.

I've learned that living in the untouchable high tower of perfectionism is unbearably lonely, where I stay terrified that I'll never belong. It's the glossy, well-manicured outside that's the front that people can't really connect with without everyone feeling "fake."

So instead of feeling connected, trying to be perfect all of the time actually makes me wonder which version of me people are drawn to — true me or perfect me.

And if the facade slips, is it all over?

Then will I be alone (again)?

But, hey, perfectionism, I see your intention. You've just been trying to protect me. (Imperfectly so, I might add!) So thank you for your attempts, but your protection is actually a smoke screen. Honestly, it comes at much too high of a cost.

More and more, I've been setting the armor down so that I can find the true me. It can feel terrifying, but when I do it, it's freaking liberating! I've had a little taste of true connection — with myself and with my people — and I kinda like it. A LOT.

I know you'll still be around from time to time, but we need to talk about our relationship now. Instead of being roommates, I'm going to insist that we become "Hi, Neighbors." You know, we'll see each other from across the street as we enter our garage, give each other a nod, and say "Hi, Neighbor."

And stay off my lawn.

But most importantly, you no longer get to be the boss of me! I'm imperfect. And I'm enough!

A Postscript to Impostor Syndrome:

I've noticed that you hang around quite a bit with Perfectionism. It seems like you're best buds, but you're actually a completely different animal.

In reality, you also hang out with Comparison and the Patriarchy in the back alley, whispering poisonous messages in my ear that keep me always questioning myself and shrinking in my own skin.

And where, with perfectionism, I can at least look back and see the feeble attempt to keep me safe, I can't extend the same generosity to you, Impostor Syndrome. Your intention is much more sinister.

You mean to "keep me in my place."

To keep me from having a seat at the table.

No number of degrees or certifications is enough.

The years of experience that I've amassed don't matter to you.

The quality of the work I do is not even taken into consideration.

Each time I try to present these as evidence to you, you slyly reply that THIS time the cat will be out of the bag, and I'll be exposed for the fraud that you say I am.

But I'm onto you. I'm not playing your game anymore.

Simply put —

There are important things I'm meant to do in my life, and you're keeping me from doing them.

I belong. And I'm enough.
End of conversation.
You can return to your back ally now.

Let's Stop Apologizing for Being Human

I was wiping down the bike after a long ride and looked down to see a huge sweat patch across my crotch.

"Oh, that's embarrassing."

The thought was completely automatic. But it also stopped me in my tracks.

I had just worked hard for 45 minutes. Sweat was dripping from my hair, ears, nose, and arms. I had to clean up a puddle of sweat from the mat under the bike.

I had worked hard to earn every bit of that sweat and was proud of every drop.

Except for the drops that had accumulated at my crotch.

I remember overhearing two women talking at a hot yoga studio about someone they saw who "sweat too much."

AT A HOT YOGA STUDIO!

If ever there is a time and place to sweat, this is it.

But somehow, our society has conditioned women to be ashamed of sweating. Bring home the bacon, fry it up in a pan, and look sexy while doing it, but never let them see you sweat. Gross. The patriarchy is pervasive. And if you think that's an exaggeration, ask yourself when the last time was that you heard a man express concern about ball sweat. Yep, that's not going to happen.

We've bought the lie that we, as women, aren't allowed to be human and take up space, much less sweat in our crotch area.

I noticed it recently during a training for therapists that I led.

"I'm sorry, I have a question." Not just once but every time she raised her hand.

I finally replied, "Stop apologizing. You paid a lot of money to be here and ask questions. I don't expect you to know all of this without doing so."

Other times, clients will apologize for being angry about a situation we're talking about, or for crying. Because if we get angry, then we're a bitch, and if we cry, we're dramatic. Then, there are the apologies for having to go to the bathroom.

We get to be human.

I say it regularly to clients, and, each time I do, it's a reminder to myself.

I'm allowed to be human, which means that I

- Sweat
- Urinate
- Defecate
- Get hungry
- Get thirsty
- Get angry
- Get lonely
- Get tired
- Have questions
- Have opinions
- Get turned on
- Get turned off
- Need support

- Need alone time
- Need connection

I'm also allowed to take up space. To have any size body. To have any sized breasts, hips, thighs, or ass. To clothe that body in ways that feel good for me. To move and nourish my body in ways that feel good and healthy, and respectful to me.

I'm allowed to wear my hair long, short, shaved, straight, curly, natural, dyed, in dreads, covered with a hat, scarf, wig, or with extensions.

I'm allowed to take up mental space and own my thoughts and unique mental brilliance.

Because we each have our own amazing way of perceiving, experiencing, and interpreting the world around us.

I'm allowed to take up emotional space. To have big feelings (or not). To laugh, cry, get angry, get annoyed, get curious.

I'm allowed to change what I want about anything. I am allowed to explore and understand the things that work for me and the things that don't. To learn and grow from this process.

To live out what it means to embrace the entirety of myself and the freedom and power that comes from that.

I might choose to explain my hot, sweaty workout. My need for food, drink, or the bathroom.

I might decide to share my opinion, my inspiration for why I dress, or how I feel.

But I don't need to apologize for it.

Neither do you.

And since we're so accustomed to doing it- oftentimes not even aware that we are - let's start by noticing the times we apologize for being human. You might be surprised at how ingrained it is for you.

I know I was.

Think about your experiences of apologizing for being human. You might not actually apologize out loud, but you shrink in your body. Make excuses. Feel awkward. Compare what you're capable of doing to others.

If you're a highly sensitive introvert like me, think about the times you forced yourself to stay in social situations that were uncomfortable and exhausting beyond any point of benefit.

Think of the times you've dismissed your need to step away from your desk. To get something to eat or drink. To move your body. "After I'm done with this task," turns into the next, then the next, then the next. Before you know it, you've been chained to the desk for hours on end.

Or think of how you apologized before putting a limit on someone's request – to move forward a deadline, to work past the end of your business day, to do or say something that didn't resonate for you.

Truly pause at this moment and think of the times that you didn't allow yourself to be human. When you regularly sacrificed sleep to get things done. When you delayed going to the bathroom. When you ate your lunch at your desk, again, instead of stepping away from work to truly nourish your body and your mind, so that you could return refreshed. How often do you make do by substituting vending machine food for something more nourishing so that you could save time? How different would your life be if you actually acknowledged and honored your physical, human limitations instead of apologizing for them?

How different would our planet be if we all did so? If we didn't try to survive on half the sleep that our bodies and minds actually need. If we put the screens away and connected over a meal? If we allowed ourselves to be human?

You Are Not a Robot

"I used to work seven days a week, but now I'm so unfocused and unmotivated."

The words hit me so hard that they threw my body back on my chair, my hands to the top of my head (yes, I might have a flair for the dramatic, but I'm *not* over-exaggerating on this one).

I quickly realized that the shock I was feeling wasn't as much about what my client was saying as it was about how I saw myself in what she said.

It was also a startling reminder that these are the hyper-capitalistic, patriarchal waters that we swim in.

We live in a society where productivity is valued and celebrated. Corporate America expects you to work an 80-hour week (plus!!). As an entrepreneur, the expectations we put on ourselves can far exceed this. I have been my own worst boss. We're in such hustle mode that we don't even take our paid vacation.

And we're dying because of it. Literally, our bodies are paying the price with medical issues. *Too bad companies don't announce how many of their employees die from heart attacks when they post their quarterly earnings.*

Our relationships are dying because work is suffocating what little quality time we might have. Our hearts are locked away in our corner office so that we continue to tell ourselves that everything is ok. It's not.

It starts early on, too. Get good grades in school. Win the awards. We're not explicitly told that our value is tied to our productivity, but we hear the implicit message at the center of our being.

The hustle takes us through college, maybe even grad school. We climb the corporate ladder, and "success" feels good. And it pays well. All of that hard work has finally paid off. The money and prestige feel damn good. Until we realize the prison that's been built around us and how treacherous the ladder of success really is. We work more and more hours because the threat of financial insecurity feels overwhelming if we don't. We take on more and more projects at work because we have to prove to the men in our office (and ourselves) that we deserve to be there.

Then, when it all begins to feel unbearable, instead of looking at the polluted waters we're swimming in, we beat ourselves up. We tell ourselves that if we weren't so "lazy", we'd be able to get our act together and be productive again (and finally get that corner office). This is the beginning of a shame spiral, where we compound our internal narrative about how we suck as a human beings. I know that I'm in a shame spiral when I feel like I've been punched in the gut, I have a cold sweat going on over my body, I wish the earth would open up and swallow me, and I think, "What have I done now to fuck things up and how do I fix it?"

By the way, I've usually done nothing more than be human.

So if we would just stop sleeping and eating and moving our bodies and investing in our relationships and play, we could find the "tools" to reach the next level of productivity. THEN our worth and value would be indispensable.

But it never is.

According to corporate America, we're all completely dispensable.

I remember when the seed was planted when I got an A- in a class and was asked why it wasn't an A+. I got a C in Geometry and was afraid I would be told to leave. That C would be the final straw to prove that I'd never be able to get my shit together enough to belong in the home, where there wasn't much attention paid to who I was, but there certainly were targeted eyes on what I did (because, well, we do what we know – and change is uncomfortable).

I swallowed that seed whole, and it took root. Watch me jump through the hoops. Watch me berate myself for being salutatorian and for not winning the Senior Class presidential election.

I remember my parents calling me during my first semester of college and telling me that it was ok to leave my dorm room from time to time – to take a break from studying and have fun. I heard them say that, but also knew what would happen if I didn't get the grades.

So I got the grades.

Watch me graduate with honors and ace an accelerated master's program.

Soul Sabbatical

I remember starting my counseling business. I checked all of the boxes to make sure I was doing it the "right" way.

Watch me contort myself to see everyone who called me at all hours of the day and evening, without regard to myself or my family's needs. As long as the hours were filled and I was being "productive."

I have the blessing and the curse that my body and heart could only swim in these waters for so long. Chronic health conditions and a propensity to a highly sensitive nervous system caused me to pause and take notice. Mostly because my body was shutting down from pain and exhaustion.

I remember talking to my business coach about this idea of "work/life balance," mostly because my body and my husband were protesting the lack thereof. We literally looked up the definition of the word "hobby" because I simply could not wrap my mind around it. It took more years before I actually had a hobby.

I remember agreeing to dates with my husband and the immense anxiety I would feel when I had to turn my phone off at the movie theater. I literally had to repeat to myself, "This is what normal people do – people who are happy and have good relationships" the entire time.

I waited for the bottom to drop out, for things to fall apart because I wasn't working "hard enough" (by the way, I've come to understand that, for me, "hard enough" really means that I wasn't suffering, when I finally became so exhausted that it quieted the anxious chatter in my head).

It didn't happen. Shockingly, the bottom didn't fall out, and I started realizing that I was better at my job when I rested, and even (gasp!) played.

It's been a process to realize that I'm not a robot. There has been some real annoyance and grief around accepting that I'm a human being who requires rest and nourishment and movement and connection and play and creativity. I hate that I am limited by the time and space continuum and can't find (magically) more than 24 hours a day. It pisses me off.

I do ok with this understanding for a while, then something happens that dunks me back into the water again. The business grows, or COVID hits, and I'm forced to problem solve, pivot, and hustle and still be reminded that I'm still very human. UGH.

> Then I tap into my humanness and take a sabbatical –
> an extended time of rest and play and connection –
> and I think for sure that the bottom will drop out.

But when I share the story, I find it's a life preserver to other women, who grab on tight and say, "I was hoping that there was a way out of these murky waters."

There is.

Instead of building more and more coping strategies, let's create lives that need fewer coping strategies.

It's time to take a break from chasing after your next big goal and chase after your own heart. Take space to see and love your own humanity.

Don't wait for the next milestone/promotion/retirement!

Burn Out:

Let's call it like it is. We are a society of the most stressed-out, anxious, exhausted, numbed-out women that America has ever housed. And we're burnt to a crisp.

Being a Florida girl, we don't have much experience with wildfires. Give us a hurricane to prepare for, and we know exactly what to do. But wildfires? They're foreign.

So, when I see a wildfire on the TV, my eyes are wide open. It's hard to comprehend the number of acres that wildfires across the western part of the country consume.

Then, to see the aftermath of a wildfire in real life is jaw-dropping. The barren land that remains scarred long after the flames are put out.

That's today's American woman. Burnt to a crisp. As we look around at the ashes, it's hard to imagine any life returning.

There are several things that contribute to burnout – and here are several from the professional arena:

- Doing work that is monotonous and unchallenging – we're bored and not inspired by what we're doing. We're stuck in the weeds.
- Too many responsibilities and not enough help from others (often because we've given the illusion that we don't need help).
- Need to control and inability to delegate, whether that's because there's no one to delegate to or because we choose not to delegate.
- (Interestingly, creativity is an antidote to burnout. Creativity is the power to connect the seemingly unconnected. We'll talk more about this later.)

But there's more beneath the waters, which we'll explore next.

Your Heart is Invited

First and foremost; your heart is invited to take care of your heart.

These are big systems to uncover, and it can feel overwhelming to truly understand how they impact you. You might feel anxious at the thought of changing some of these patterns, much less taking action to do so.

So take your time. The process is about the journey of unburdening yourself from the weight of these things. There is no timeline. You have all the time in the world to go at the pace that feels best for you.

Here are some things to consider:

In what ways have you learned to adapt to survive our society's broken systems?

Which of these things would you like to resign from?

Spend a few minutes journaling about how different systems have impacted you and identify a few things that you'd like to start doing differently.

Maybe you don't check your work email after the end of your work day. Maybe you identify an end to your workday instead of working until you go to bed.

Maybe you don't eat lunch at your desk and go for a walk around the block during an afternoon break.

Feel how your body responds to the idea of giving this a try. What do you notice?

What would get in the way of you doing the new thing? What can you put in place to remove that barrier?

Chapter 2
The Water We Swim In

I n addition to the more generally known work conditions that lead to burnout, we are dealing with more implicit conditions that have caused us to be here. These are the societal systems that swallow us. The rules of these systems aren't generally explicitly outlined – if they were, we would never choose to enter them! – but these are the polluted waters we swim in. Because they are the waters that we were born into, that we're surrounded by every hour of every day, it's harder to see their impact on us.

Quite likely, you're getting a sense of how hyper-capitalism, the patriarchy, and how our society glorifies the hustle and over-functioning impact us. But, as a therapist, I'd like to bring to light something we rarely talk about.

These are the invisible wounds that we don't talk about. The ones to our mental, emotional, and spiritual psyche. Those of us in the field of mental health call these wounds trauma. They encapsulate the "Big T" experiences like assault, combat, and natural disaster. These are the experiences that we most readily identify as trauma. But there are also experiences that don't seem as extreme but still leave scars on our hearts, minds, and souls. These are the relational wounds that impact our behaviors. They're usually not one big event but several smaller and eternally ongoing experiences. Think death by a thousand paper cuts.

And the death? It's the connection to our value and worth. Our sense of belonging and safety in the world.

And the way that we don't bother getting to know ourselves...

Until now.

"What is it you plan to do with your one wild and precious life?"

— Mary Oliver

FOOBS Fighting

I was sitting with a group of friends not long ago – fellow therapist entrepreneurs who are simply kick-ass, amazing people. Not only are they genius and super savvy business people, but they are also next-level therapists with a passion for guiding people to healing. They're strong, funny, witty, creative, and so inventive. We are both like-minded and different enough to resonate with and challenge each other simultaneously. I just delight in being with them, and we prioritize in-person business retreats several times a year to spend time together. When we're together, we mastermind business stuff, laugh, cry, eat good food, drink good drinks, and usually hike. A lot. I can't tell you how much I adore them.

The last time we were together, our conversation shifted from business to personal, as it tends to do. We know and trust one another, so usually, there is nothing off-limits in our conversations. Every therapist has a story about what led them into the field, and we were sharing our stories. And every single one of our stories was about our childhood wounds.

In my trauma therapy practice, we use the acronym FOOBS – family of origin bullshit. It's our colloquial term for another acronym, ACES – Adverse Childhood Experiences, which is a long-standing study about the effects of childhood trauma like physical and sexual abuse, emotional and physical neglect, parental substance abuse, mental health problems, divorce/separation, and incarceration, among other markers.

You might not think of yourself as having experienced trauma because most of us think of "Big T" trauma when we hear the word. But take a look at what "little t," or relational trauma, looks like (and these often leave deeper wounds emotionally, mentally, relationally, and even physically than the others that come to mind when we think of trauma).

It's growing up in an environment where we didn't feel

- Safe (physically and emotionally)
- Heard
- Seen and Understood
- Soothed and Comforted
- That we mattered.

Homes that didn't offer

- Nurture
- Guidance
- Healthy and Loving Limits

Relational Traumas that were

- Intrusive and Disempowering, like physical and verbal abuse.
- Intrusive and Falsely Empowering, like physical and emotional caretaking of a parent.
- Abandoning and Disempowering, hello, my dear Scapegoats who are the Black Sheep of the family.
- Abandoning and Falsely Empowering – a loving nod to my fellow Hero children, who carried the heavy expectations of making the family look good.

These experiences in childhood can affect our physical health throughout life, often leading to chronic health conditions like asthma, diabetes, and autoimmune conditions.

They also affect our mental and emotional health, leading us to have distorted self-view and views of the world, which causes us to question our value and can make our relationships with ourselves and others challenging.

And, when this happens, these experiences can often embed the hustle more deeply – down to a cellular and brain level.

Every single one of us had a history of these childhood experiences. Every single one of us had a history of over-hustling to our detriment. In fact, one of the benefits of us being in connection with one another is to help keep that over-hustle at bay because we know the cost of it. When I find myself sliding in the over-functioning direction, I reach out to one of them. And they know they have my permission to call me (lovingly) on it.

As we're sitting together, sharing stories about our first therapy session, where we realized and were validated that what we had actually experienced growing up was trauma that doesn't actually happen in other homes, remembering how we thought, "Oh, so this ISN'T the way it's supposed to be!", my brain starts ticking through all of the highly successful, super-driven women who have come into my office.

And their lives are unraveling.

Because they had never dealt with their FOOBS.

Because they didn't realize it was a problem. (really, they did. We just don't talk about it, and the shame of it made them think that they were the only ones. So they minimized it.)

Because they got really good at shoving it all down.

And piling the hustle and perfectionism and performing and people-pleasing on top, hoping that it would make the rest of it go away.

Or at least get smaller.

Because they were afraid to face it. Afraid of opening Pandora's Box.

Without realizing that they were LIVING in Pandora's Box.

But, since we don't talk about it, we don't realize how it's impacting us. Or that there's anything we can do about it.

I remember the first time that I went to therapy.

I had already spent a great deal of time going round and round with my medical provider after he suggested that I had depression and recommended that I go on an antidepressant.

Nope. Not here. Not me.

I was living the American dream, a stay-at-home mom at the time, happily married with three healthy kids. The house with the white picket fence. The dog, the cat, and the family dinner around the table every night.

What did I have to be depressed about?

There was a moment when I was complaining about how tired I was, how it felt like I was dragging my body through quicksand, how annoyed I was by my husband, the kids, and on and on to a friend one morning at the gym. She mentioned the whole depression thing. I pushed back against her, too.

"That's ok. You're not in enough pain yet."

What. The. Actual. Fuck?

That complete (loving) slap-in-the-face moment was my wake-up call to get my ass back to the doctor for the meds.

And while I was at it, try out therapy. Someone that I knew at the time was completing her Master's degree and needed clinical hours for school, so I agreed to meet with her.

I (very mistakenly) thought that the appointment was going to be like regular girl talk until she announced,

"So, you grew up in an alcoholic, abusive household."

My eyes darted around the room that the oxygen was just sucked out of, and I thought.

"We don't say that out loud."

(PS, this was the moment that I knew I had to become a therapist.)

Since this moment, through further therapy and formal training, I began to link this truth to its lasting impact into my adulthood.

How those Adverse Childhood Experiences led to chronic headaches and other odd medical things through childhood and chronic health issues and autoimmune conditions that still exist.

How I had internalized those degrading, shaming messages from childhood and how they impacted my ability to show up healthy in my relationship and contributed to my depression.

How I had spent a lifetime walking on eggshells and performing in an effort to stay out of the bullseye and safe had translated to super-hyper-perfectionist hustle at all costs to myself.

How my perpetually hunched shoulders had less to do with my posture (and wouldn't be helped by those horrid posture bras that I was told to wear as a teen) and had everything to do with the fact that I was protecting my heart.

And why is it, decades after the first ACEs study that gives the things that happened in our childhood context to how we show up as adults, that we're still not talking about it?

Which is why I'm writing about it here.

Our childhood leaves an impression on us, and yours DOES impact you.

And there's something you can do about it.

Your Unexplored Inner Landscape

"What do you do when life isn't working?"

It was a question from a client that I was meeting with for the first time. She had been hugely successful in her business. She had the look of success with everything that goes along with it. Except that she is scared every moment of every day that it will all fall apart.

It's a feeling that's familiar to many of us. And one that we stay tied to until we're brave enough to explore the depths of our inner landscape.

To be honest, the thought of exploring the depths of who we are is similar to a hike that my husband and I went on recently through the wetlands of a Florida campground.

It was a bit intimidating.

The trail was marked as "difficult."

The sign described the wetlands that the trail weaved through as being perceived as "dangerous" and "unuseful."

Soul Sabbatical

But the invitation of the trail was to make our way through "difficult."

To walk into the "dangerous" and "unuseful" to explore.

The beauty.

The strength.

The complexity.

To see beyond the intimidating and actually experience the birds. The butterflies. The botany. And that sky.

And it made me think of how we treat our own internal wetland landscapes.

The parts of us that feel too dangerous and unuseful to explore (because, honestly, do I really want to see that side of myself?)

Too big.

Too small.

Too loud.

Too quiet.

Too needy.

Too confident.

And how avoiding these trails keeps us from understanding the depth and complexity of our own ecosphere.

How light can't function without the dark?

How are there no parts of us that are unworthy?

How can we invite these parts of ourselves back from exile?

And walk with them, hand in hand.

Yolanda Harper

And see their beauty.

The beauty that is us.

"Only the paradox comes anywhere near to comprehending the fullness of life."

— *Carl Yung*

This is the space of the paradox, where light and darkness weave through our hearts. One is incomplete without the other. It's the exploration of our shadow parts – those that we wish weren't there. The parts of ourselves that we abandon because they're not shiny and glossy.

Can I tell you a secret?

Lean in...

A little closer...

Abandoning them doesn't make them go away (deep down, you already knew this).

Also, shaming them and exiling them doesn't make them go away, either (you also knew this).

It just makes you react from those spaces. Even (and especially) though you don't want to.

So all of the times that you do or say something and then say, "Where did THAT come from?"

Meet your unexplored shadow wetlands.

Really. They're actually dangerous and unuseful only when left unexplored. When we have a better understanding of our shadow side, we can step ahead of it and correct it. Lovingly.

And even with some humor.

"Shadow work is the path of the heart warrior"

— *Carl Yung*

I call my shadow self part of me – the one that acts out with cringey behavior and leaves relational wreckage all over the place – Linda. You know, like the "Listen, Linda!" video with the kid from several years ago (Google it. Really!)

I've developed a relationship with Linda. I get where she's coming from. She's just been trying to protect me. I appreciate her. Have compassion for the suffering she's endured. I know why she learned to hustle and people please, where she learned to come across as big and scary when she's afraid. And, also, I know she's not the wisest part of me. So sometimes, I have to firmly remind her to "Listen, Linda!"

My conversations with her go something like this:

Dear Linda (aka, my Hustle, Heartbroken Self) – The Most Tender Letter to My Own Heart

I see you and all the things you had to endure... how you learned to be really small and quiet so that you didn't draw attention to yourself.

How confusing it was when you were in the center of the bulls-eye. How you didn't understand the chaos and rage. It was like a tidal wave that crashed against your body– sometimes in actual blows. The seething words might as well have been blows. You carried the shame and humiliation in your body (in many ways, you still do).

You learned to walk on eggshells and not trust. You were told that the people who were hurting you were the most trustworthy people you'd meet in your life, while you had great mistrust for the people who wanted to help.

You were taught to believe that, and it was a mind-fuck. It made you question everything your heart and wisdom told you.

That wasn't okay. You should have felt safe in your own home. Your birthright was to be loved without condition — not trying to calculate every misstep against being a "Good Girl" and never understanding that math.

You should have been looked at with eyes of deep love, acceptance, and belonging.

You should have had ample experiences of feeling
Safe
Heard
Seen, and understood
That you mattered.

Instead, there was pain.

It wasn't ok to be hit with hands or belts or words. It wasn't okay to be humiliated to tears and then be told that if you didn't stop crying, then you would be given something to cry about.

And those empty spots in your memory? Those things weren't okay, either.

But these are the things you have given me...

A strong work ethic. A great sense of loyalty (that I'm learning to direct toward the appropriate people). You gave me an incredible sense of empathy and compassion (even toward the people who hurt you who were truly doing the best they could). You taught me how to perspective-take and honed in me a sense of justice.

But you've also cost me a lot. Too much.
I've struggled to understand that I must be as kind to myself as I am to others. I didn't have a sense of belonging or self-respect. You've caused me to work beyond exhaustion because I believed that I was valuable only for the things I did, not who I was.

And the exhaustion didn't produce the results that were expected. There was always something more to do. Better. The A wasn't good enough... Why wasn't it an A+?
(why wasn't it ever enough?)

You nearly wrecked my relationships. As much as I tried to protect my kids from the rage that you learned to unleash when you had finally had enough, that still came out more than it ever should have. I put the same dumb, unrealistic expectations on them and shamed them, and that's not okay.

You put such a strain on my marriage by putting my beloved in the same category as those who hurt you. You shut down your heart behind the icy wall, then raged. You learned to shut down to protect yourself, then reenacted the rage. Then you swam in shame for acting in the ways you never thought you would.

Hiding in your ice cave made people think that you were unapproachable. Because you were. You didn't want to be, but you didn't know any other way to protect yourself.

Those that did make it through the icy walls unintentionally pushed your people-pleasing buttons so that you gave and gave and gave and gave and gave and gave and gave until you were completely tapped out and resentful.

Thank God for time and love and healing and forgiveness.

You see, there are new ways to practice. New ways to live. There is redemption.

I get that you were just trying to protect the scared, lonely me that sat properly on the couch with the frilly dress and the patent shoes, looking just like that porcelain doll that sat on your shelf that you weren't allowed to play with.

You were trying so desperately to protect the me that was beaten for riding her bike with her sister. The one that sobbed as she was forced to do push-ups and wall sits, being yelled at and berated for something she didn't understand.

You were counting the number of beer cans that were stacked on the living room floor.

You were keeping a tally of the times that there was no accountability for hurtful words and behavior. (How *did nobody see it? They did. Nobody DID anything about it.)*

You were counting down the number of days before you could leave.

But things are different now.

The people who did those things are not as big and scary. They've also changed. They try harder not to be hurtful. When they are, they're more likely to take accountability. To ask for forgiveness. To make amends.

You've let your heart grow and have a wisdom that was formed in this fire. It's been the scariest and best thing that you've ever done in your life. You never would have chosen this growth, but you're glad it chose you. The love that you've received and that you now give to yourself and others can be trusted beyond all else.

Linda, when you start getting freaked out about what's happening, know that I'm here. Just grab my hand. I'll take the time to hear your worries and tell you how I'll protect you.

Then I'll give you a big hug and let you know that being freaked out is understandable. You'll get behind me (and the other big, beautiful, and safe hearts that are in your life) and know that you're protected.

You get to relax now. There's love and happiness here.

Belonging to Yourself

Getting an understanding of our interior landscape is the epitome of the Hero's Journey. If you're unfamiliar with the concept of Joseph Campbell's monomyth, think of every example of any enduring story that you love, from Star Wars to The Wizard of Oz, Lord of the Rings, Inside Out, The Hunger Games... the list goes on and on. Here the heroine leaves the world that is familiar to her as she is called into a great adventure. After she fights, then accepts the call, she learns to navigate the new world, and in it, she approaches the innermost cave. Only after meeting and befriending the shadow parts of herself can the heroine return home, a stronger, more integrated version of herself.

As we enter into our own innermost cave/landscape, we meet the orphaned, exiled parts of ourselves. The parts that are wounded and fragile. The ones that have learned to adapt in maladaptive ways.

As we draw our "Lindas" onto our laps and wrap our arms around the wounded parts of ourselves, and as we firmly remind these parts that they no longer get to run the show, we come home to ourselves more and more.

We experience a true sense of belonging in our own skin because we know that no one part of us defines our entirety. We no longer feel the need to hustle and perform and people please in order to fit in; rather, we understand that no one belongs more than we do.

Your Heart is Invited:

Write a letter to the most tender, orphaned, shadow parts of yourself using this format.

Yolanda Harper

Dear _____

Thank you for all you have done for me in my life. This is how you protected me...

These are the things you have given to me...

These are the things you have cost me.

There are wiser parts of me here now. I can take care of both of us. I'm at the wheel, and this is what it's going to look like now...

Then sign it, love, (your name)

Chapter 3
Your Heart Has Been Swimming In...Your Heart is Invited To...

Yolanda Harper

Recognizing the systemic and behavioral waters you've been swimming in and listening to the invitation of your heart is the beginning of a better understanding of yourself and of healing.

As we've become a society of performance and outcome, we've come to value "knowing" above all else. We privilege our thinking over feeling. In a way, this makes sense because "knowing" takes away uncertainty. "Knowing" increases productivity and status. Aren't we all wanting to be the "expert" in our field?

Even in the therapy world, there has been a focus on thoughts above feelings with modalities like Cognitive Behavioral Therapy, i.e., let me understand how my thoughts impact my emotions and behaviors so that I can bypass the messy emotional piece and hack the system.

As a therapist, for the longest time I tried to pretend that the work that I do isn't "Tell me about your childhood" and "How does that make you feel?"

Then, I had to be honest with myself that this is exactly the work I do because it's the deep, meaningful, most impactful work that we as humans can do.

But let me tell you, we are painfully unconnected with our emotional selves. Anything beyond the top-three – mad, sad, glad – we struggle with.

Our hearts have been swimming in feelings, emotions, and experiences that are much more complex than mad, sad, or glad, however. Like a duck, we look calm on the surface-but until we can name them and work through them, we're actually paddling frantically below.

Without recognizing and working through more complex emotional experiences, we continue to react in the same old ways. Understanding our emotions and the wisdom we can glean from them gives us a pathway to respond from a more centered place.

Have you noticed how we are always swimming in the waters of worry, anxiety, and stress?

Like literally swimming in this.

Close your eyes for a second and picture yourself in water up to your neck right now, and the water around you is made up of worry, anxiety, and stress. This water is like the frog in the pot, where the temperature is turned up bit by bit until it's boiling. The water is slimy and sticky and smells like a swamp. You feel heavy trying to move through it, and each time you try to take a breath, your chest tightens.

It starts with a moment of worry – a negative thought about bad things that might happen in the future.

I'm not going to make my numbers for this month.

That client will leave.

My partner and I will get into another nasty argument.

I'll get another call from the school about my kid misbehaving.

I'm going to blow that presentation that I've been working so hard on.

The test results will confirm that diagnosis.

When I feel tension and physical changes, like the whoosh in my body of my blood pressure increasing, the pounding in my ears of my heart racing, my stomach clenching, my sweaty palms – this is what stress feels like in my body. When I start having a hard time sleeping because of the worried thoughts – that's anxiety (you know this one, right?)

But because I've become so accustomed to feeling this perpetually, I keep plugging along. Hell, I DOUBLE DOWN on getting shit done because isn't that how you're supposed to respond to worry and anxiety? By over-functioning? Hell, isn't the energy of the worry and anxiety what fuels the getting shit done?

SURE!

(Oh, by the way, steamrolling through all of these worries and anxiety leaves me exhausted. And makes me act like a snarky, entitled brat who lashes out on said partner and kid and friend and teammate and... but maybe that's just me...)

At this point, I'm stressed to the max, and although I would never admit it out loud, I'm starting to feel overloaded and beginning to wonder if all of these demands are outpacing my ability to cope successfully. Also, even if I DID admit it out loud, would anyone take it seriously since everyone knows me as the queen of getting through hard things?

I'm questioning my ability to handle it all.

I'm in the weeds, and the volume on my "Itty Bitty Shitty Committee" is full blasting me with all of those rote messages of:

What's wrong with me?

I should be able to handle this.

If I were a better wife/mom/professional/friend/etc., this wouldn't be a problem.

And the last thing I intend to do is raise the white flag. In fact, I'm more than doubling down to fix the problem.

But secretly, inside, I'm wondering how much I have left in me; Until overwhelm.

A complete shutdown, then I have nothing left. (PS, this is usually reserved for the weekend. We call it "crashing," so we can get up and do it again Monday morning. No wonder we have the "Sunday Saddies" when the weekend all-too-quickly comes to an end.)

Or, maybe, you're swimming in waters of comparison, envy, jealousy, resentment, and perfectionism.

Because those are calm and soothing water, right? - NOT!

Hmm, how does this one start?

I start by comparing myself to someone.

Their career.

Their accomplishments.

How they're being asked to speak. Or traveling the world for their work. Or raking in the big bucks.

Or how they've just had an amazing vacation with their partner, where clearly they're having the time of their lives, getting along perfectly, eating great food, and having great sex.

Or their kid just won a scholarship and found the cure for cancer... or something like that.

And I want to be just... like... them...

But Better.

The comparison is caused by (or leads to, it can go either way)

Envy – why can't I have that? What do I need to do to get that? I want that!

Or

Jealousy – How will I keep up if I lose what I have? You can't have what I have – it's mine!

And it spins up my perfectionism.

Perfectionism is my addiction. Seriously, I'm actively in recovery. And, like any recovery, some days are better than others.

I like to believe that perfectionism moves me towards getting what I want, but really it's my desperate attempt to protect myself from shame, judgment, and blame (usually self-imposed!).

When perfectionism doesn't work, because I'm human and it's not a thing anyway, I don't stop and think, "Hey, maybe this perfectionism route isn't the way to go." I think, "I'll just be MORE perfect next time!" Because that makes perfect sense, right? And the cycle spirals on and on.

Perfectionism usually leads to resentment, which, surprisingly, is part of the envy family.

This is how resentment works...

I'm angry that I'm working so hard at something that, clearly, the other person is not putting ample effort into it. This makes me snarky and keeps the focus on the other person instead of looking at myself to see what boundaries I need to put in place or how I can ask for support instead of trying to control how others think, feel, and react.

The Comparison -> Resentment -> Scarcity Equation

The biggest problem with comparison and resentment is the scarcity fallacy that it puts me in. I start to see life as some zero-sum game. If someone gets something, that means I don't get it

– or worse, they've taken it from me. The competition leads me to act in ways that aren't congruent with my values, trying to figure out how to take the other person out instead of creating community and collaboration, which is what actually fuels and sustains me.

All of it makes me shrink, get small, and isolate. And that absence of meaningful connection is lonely. This is a big part of why we have a national epidemic of loneliness. And, between the increased physical risks like stroke and heart disease and the increased mental health factors that contribute to increased suicide, loneliness is deadly water to swim in.

The Big Three:

1. Vulnerability
2. Grief
3. Shame

I'll admit - these are a bit cringey. They're the emotions and experiences that we all live, and NOBODY wants to talk about. But talk about them, we must. These are full-contact emotions. They're called feelings because we feel them in our body, and these we feel especially so.

Vulnerability

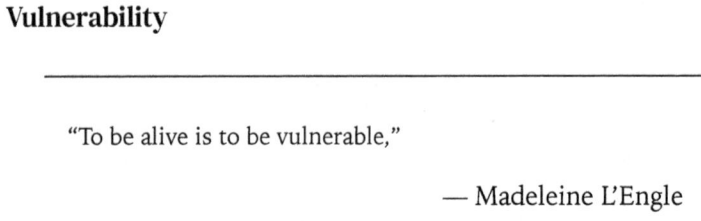

"To be alive is to be vulnerable,"

— Madeleine L'Engle

Let's start with the one that I probably identify with the most – Vulnerability.

Vulnerability is what I experience during times of uncertainty, risk, and emotional exposure. I pretty much recognize a feeling of vulnerability every single day.

When I ask for help.

When I'm waiting for the test results from the doctor.

When I say "I love you" first.

When I have a difficult conversation with my partner.

When I try something new.

When I speak my truth (and write a book).

When I explore my deepest desires and dreams.

Basically, any time I allow myself to feel and where I'm not 100% sure of the outcome, I'm in vulnerability.

So why even bother with vulnerability?

Because it's the beginning of courage and connection. It's what I move through to live a more meaningful life. It's how I find my purpose.

Soul Sabbatical

It feels a lot like fear, but there's also a pull in it. A draw for me because I know of the good things that are on the other side.

Yolanda Harper

Grief, Loss, Longing, and Feeling Lost.

"The risk of love is loss, and the price of loss is grief - But the pain of grief is only a shadow when compared with the pain of never risking love."

— *Hillary Stanton Zunin*

These are all our human attempts to reaffirm or reconstruct a world of meaning that has been challenged by loss.

And our society is swimming in grief in a way that we haven't experienced in our lifetime, not just because of the physical deaths resulting from COVID-19 but also a very real sense of longing for some aspects of "the way life used to be" and a sense of feeling lost as we attempt to bravely create new social justice structures and a new equitable way of working.

Our society doesn't do grief. If I'm grieving, I might give myself permission to do so for about five minutes, then there's a sense of pressure to "get over it" and get back in the game. Your friends and family might whisper behind your back about how it's been six months already and how they're worried that you're stuck in the past. And grief at work? Forget about it. There's no crying at work.

But grief doesn't operate like that. I know I'm in grief when I have a fuzzy, confused sense in my head, "What's going on here?" and I feel waves upon waves crashing over me – a punch in the gut, a grip on my heart, a feeling of being ungrounded and untethered.

It feels big because it's important.

Soul Sabbatical

And you have to learn to ride the wave.

Otherwise, it metastasizes.

Deep into your bones and your heart and your soul.

There have been big losses in life. Of innocence. Of the old, comfortable way of doing things. Of people I've loved. Of roles that I've played that I no longer do.

As I've stayed present to my grief, I notice that it lessens bit by bit over time. It gives me a more pure connection to the one I've lost or the thing I'm longing for (like an unrealized dream). It helps me to learn more about myself and be present with others who are grieving.

Grief is deep, soulful, spiritual work that can't be and won't be hacked by a process but will demand the time and respect that it deserves. Our hearts won't have it any other way.

Shame - the WWF Smack-Down of all Emotions

"We can endure all kinds of pain. It's shame that eats men whole,"

— Leigh Bardugo.

Shame.

Just seeing the word on the page feels icky.

When I experience it, I'm down for the count. Over the years, I've learned that I'm not fit for human consumption when I'm in shame – meaning, I'm likely to do or say something that I will later regret.

I liken myself to a wounded dog when I experience shame.

I'm in the corner, licking my wound, and if you try to approach me, you'll likely be attacked.

Shame is a full-body experience for me – time slows down, I have a heaviness in the pit of my stomach, a cold sweat, and my armpits are tingly. I want the ground to open up and swallow me, and my automatic thought is, "what did I do to fuck things up this time, and how do I fix it?"

Why all the fuss?

Shame is inherently tied to our value, worth, and sense of belonging.

This is how we get guilt and shame mixed up so often in our society because guilt has a focus on behavior... I did something that's not in alignment with my values or the person I'm striving to be, but shame is a focus on identity... I am bad.

So, while I might accurately say, "I feel guilty for not calling my mom when I told her I would," because the behavior of not following through with a commitment is incongruent with my value, the more implicit message I'm giving myself is, "I'm such a lousy human being. What kind of daughter forgets to call her mother back? I suck!"

Before I know it, that internal message of "I suck as a human being" has translated into all parts of my life – and body – and I'm hustling and perfecting and people-pleasing to get ahead of it.

Sidenote: Those of us with difficult "early learnings," those adverse childhood experiences, that relational trauma, have more highly correlated experiences of shame. The water that we swim in has seeped into every cell in our bodies because, from a child's point of view, I must be a bad person for bad things to happen to me. I must not have deserved someone to protect me. I'm so bad that not even the people who were supposed to protect me did. In fact, I'm so bad that they're the ones who hurt me.

This experience seeps into our souls, and we can experience our spirituality from a sense of shame, of God punishing me because I'm a bad person and have done something horrible to deserve this pain. I wait on a razor's edge for a bolt of lightning to be hurled from the sky to obliterate me. And, if something good happens, it is only a matter of time before it will be ripped from my desperate grasp.

As I learned to recognize what shame feels like, I started to get a better understanding of what triggers my shame – everything from my identity as a "good enough" therapist, entrepreneur, wife, mom, and friend to if my body is the right size and shape, how fat my bank account is, and whether or not I'm being "generous enough" with my time and talent as a helping professional.

Only then could I start to fact-check my expectations of myself and reach out to speak shame (after I've spent some time holding myself kindly and calming my nervous system and shame's fight/flight/freeze/fix/fawn response).

Only then could I get a handle on shame and not viciously attack myself or those around me. To not bully myself or others. To not engage in the unhealthy behaviors of over-working and over-eating and overspending, and isolating (and all of the others) that come along with the feeling of shame.

For a change.

And isn't it time to come out of attack mode?

Let's Get Real

Let me be explicitly clear about emotions. The idea here is NOT to eradicate these difficult emotions, as much as we like that idea.

There will be the heat of rage as you work through anger. You are not your anger.

There will be tears. Your tears are SACRED.

Read that again.

Sacred.

I've always been a crier. I've never been able not to cry, even when my tears were met with others' anger and humiliation. I used to hate the fact that I couldn't keep from crying. Now, I see that every single tear serves a purpose and is valuable. I honor each one and what it teaches me. I have a ritual of folding up empty tissue boxes and thanking them for their service.

Maybe you're not there. You hate to cry. To be honest, I don't LOVE it, either, but I do respect it. It doesn't mean you're weak. It shows a different kind of strength. One that society doesn't applaud but that our heart does.

The idea is to feel our feelings and learn from them in order to live a more embodied life. This is the practice and awareness that is necessary to realign what we do with what we believe in.

This is where our heart's invitation is. Let's see what it looks like to open the invitation from your heart.

Your Heart is Invited... (the things your heart has been crying out for)

My journey to my Soul Sabbatical started with head knowledge.

An understanding.

A wake-up call to the breadth and depth of what we are living as women in this country. As I took in this information in my mind, I began to awaken to the strong, desperate emotions that I'd been storing deep in my body and soul.

But I also knew that I was being called to something more. Something beyond the murky waters surrounding me.

Once I could recognize, be present to, and move through the dark waters that my heart has been marinating in, I found an expansiveness of emotions, feelings, and experiences.

It started with a sense of curiosity, having a presence with myself, with no agenda other than to deepen my relationship with the most important person in my life –me. When I slowed down, I began to recognize and tolerate the paradox, realizing that things can seem to be a contradiction, but are very much connected.

Like how anxiety and excitement feel the same in the body – the sole difference is how I choose to interpret the experience. So, instead of telling myself that I was too anxious to be present for what might come up, I told myself that I was excited and curious to know myself better.

As I showed up for myself, I was able to teach myself that I was listening. I felt deeply seen, heard, and valued by myself. I met myself with respect, kindness, and affection, practicing non-judgment. This was challenging, at times, because so much of that critical voice is innate in me, but in doing so, I learned to love and belong to myself.

The heart of this belonging work is making space. This space is our power. Choice. Learning. Our inability to access this healing space serves all of the existing systems. It's time for a new system.

Looking in the mirror at only my Hustle Me gave me such a faulty view of myself. As I practiced loving myself, I could meet myself with a sense of awe, wishing to understand myself more and wonder, desiring this unfiltered me to shine more brightly. I could more clearly see Healthy Me.

I'm able to live from a place of healthy boundaries, where I can love others and myself equally and simultaneously instead of prioritizing others until I get resentful, crash, and burn.

I find that I have greater access to feelings of joy, deep spiritual connection, pleasure, and appreciation for things. I'm a bit calmer during difficulties (I call this serenity under duress, a practice of equanimity). I can more easily access feelings of contentment, feeling satisfied, and tranquility. I carry a sense of gratitude for what is instead of being depleted by my sense of what I don't have.

I don't have all of these all of the time. But I have them more than I did yesterday. And because it's a lifelong journey, I'll have access to more tomorrow than I do today.

Meet Hope

I don't remember ever having a formal introduction to Hope, but as I look back, she has been around all along, with her loyal companions, Faith and Love, by her side.

And just like Faith and Love require action on my part to be in a relationship, so does Hope. Hope is a blending of head and heart. Hope starts with me setting a goal:

To leave a Love Legacy by loving myself and others more purely.

Hope shows me that there are several paths that I can take to reach this goal. If one of them doesn't work, I can stay flexible and take another path.

Hope is my biggest cheerleader, reminding me that I CAN DO THIS.

And, lest I start to believe that Hope is all rainbows and unicorns, she reminds me that she is born through adversity and discomfort.

Hope points out that all of those tears that I've shed mean something.

Hope is redemption.

Like me, you might not remember a formal introduction to Hope, but take a look back across your lifeline and see her steady presence, both in quiet moments and in Phoenix Rising accomplishments.

Because we're holding on hard to Hope, Faith, and Love for what's to come.

Your Heart is Invited: Where Is Your Heart?

Your heart is invited to question.

Why are we trying to do this new thing? To live in this counter-cultural, soul-nourishing way.

It's hard.

People won't understand.

They'll judge.

It'll make people uncomfortable.

No one else is doing it this way.

There's no way this is going to work out.

It's so vulnerable.

Let's just stop.

But when you get still with yourself, and it's quiet, you realize that it's not actually your heart talking.

It's your head.

Sometimes the heart jumps on the head's bandwagon because it's used to being carried along for the ride. (That's how it's gotten lost along the way.)

We like to think the head is the wisest part of us, but it's not.

The head's job is to keep us alive, so sometimes it tells us lies in its lizard-brain attempt to do so.

But the head isn't the wisest part of us.

The heart is.

When we listen to the heart, we find wisdom.

This new thing that we're doing is important.

It's ok to feel nervous and excited — it's called courage.

Yes, some people will judge. (They're not your true people.)

You will make some people uncomfortable.

(Their hearts are trying to talk to them, too.)

And if one of those people stops, gets quiet, and is brave enough to place a hand over their heart and listen,

it's all worth it.

What is your heart questioning? What emotions is your heart experiencing?

Part Two
Heart Check

Chapter 4
Permission to Dream

"All our dreams can come true, if we have the courage to pursue them,"

— Walt Disney

R emember when you were little, and an adult would ask you what you wanted to be when you grew up? Maybe you knew exactly what you wanted to do from a young age. Or maybe your answer changed each time you were asked. Asking a young child what they want to be when they grow up is my favorite because they don't know how to limit themselves yet. For example, a young child might tell you they want to be both an astronaut and a princess– and being both is entirely possible.

As we grow older, this possibility is stifled. We're supposed to know exactly what we want to do with the rest of our lives as we hit middle school so that we can take the "right" classes in high school, participate in the "right" sports and extracurricular activities in order to get into the "right" college. Because we don't know about the real world, we often make decisions based on others' expectations – our parents, teachers, and coaches. I spent three years studying International Relations and French with the thought of becoming an International Lawyer, not because I knew what that meant (or even, really if it was a real thing!), but because it seemed like an "important enough" title to make my parents and teachers happy. And, no, I never did finish that degree.

For most of us, the waters we swim in choke out our capacity to dream. While we do fine with identifying big life goals – where to go to school, our desired profession, how to climb the ladder of success, even goals to partner and have children (or not) are not hard to put on our to-do list. We often just take the next step that's expected of us.

But along the way, we lose our capacity to check in with our heart's desires and ask the question, "What do you want, Darling?" and to reach deeply with the response of "what if…?"

We start to doubt that our heart's yearnings are possible. Or even permissible.

Do we have the "right" to dream?

Here's the space where we reconnect. To our passions. Our truths. Our dreams.

We've been tricked into thinking that to do so is frivolous. A waste of time.

But it actually means that we're robbing the world of something truly beautiful.

Our hearts.

The Fallacy of the American Dream

Several years ago, my husband and I were having dinner with good friends. We were all entrenched in the Corporate American grind and pursuing the American Dream.

You know the classic American Dream, right? The job you retire from complete with a pension and the gold watch. The notoriety in your given industry. How that career magically blends with the idea of owning a home with a white picket fence. The 2.5 happy, healthy kids with the family dog by your side.

But that night, at dinner, our friend asked the question burning in each one of our hearts, "Is this all there is? Is this everything we've worked for? It seems like there should be, well, more…"

It was a punch in the gut. I wonder if you've felt it, too. All of this hard work – for what? Something still feels like it's missing.

Because the hustle and the grind don't take into account our hearts. The desire for something beyond the mundane 9 to 5, or whatever insane schedule you find yourself in. To not feel like you have to sacrifice decades of your life to actually live after retirement… only to be too sick to enjoy life once you get there.

There's the reality that there is no gold watch retirement from a company you've worked for for decades. No pension. If you're lucky, there's matching retirement money that you can hold on to. Most of us have very little of that, though.

There's the fallacy that we can bring home the bacon, fry it up in the pan, and never let them see us sweat. That, somehow, work-life balance exists when companies demand you to be on call every waking minute (and what's up with kids' extra-curricular activities taking the time and effort of another full-time job?).

Have you noticed this, too?

I've worked with countless clients who come to therapy because retirement life is not what they envisioned. What we hope is the payoff for sacrificing to the hustle culture is smoke and mirrors. Instead of doing what retirees thought they would enjoy, they spend their time going from one doctor to another, making up for all the years that they were too busy working to go to the doctor.

When we're caught up in hustle culture, we start to believe that we have little agency over how we spend our time and energy. That our lives are dictated by clock-punching and billable hours.

We forget that we can choose to be the author of our lives and choose what we do, when, how, and with whom.

A Perfect Day

Years ago, I was working with my business coach, Kelly Higdon, around bringing balance between my personal and entrepreneurial selves. I had the business hustle down, but it came at the cost of my health and relationships. During the conversation, we actually and for real (I'm not exaggerating) had to look up the definition of the word "hobby" because I could not fathom doing things for the pure pleasure of doing them without having some kind of self-development or business agenda behind it.

Kelly also introduced me to the Perfect Day Exercise – a journaling prompt to write out, in as much detail as possible, what an ideal day of work, play, connection, and rest would look like. This has been a game changer for me, and I spend some time doing it at least quarterly or whenever I'm feeling stuck.

As much as I wanted to dismiss the benefit of doing this as some kind of woo-hoo, "pie in the sky" thinking, I quickly realized the power of dreaming and how good it feels. How doing so unlocks a beautiful piece of you that's been shut down for so long, how it gives you permission to acknowledge things that you might dismiss as frivolous, needy, or unrealistic.

I was sitting at a stop light on my way to work one day, thinking about the Perfect Day that I had written about and realizing that being in the car, driving back and forth to work and home, and yoga and home. Back and forth. Back and forth. Those hours spent in the car weren't part of my perfect day. I hate driving. I hate traffic. Every day felt like the drive was longer, and the traffic was worse. Wouldn't it be nice to live on the other side of town, closer to the office, yoga studio, and friends, where my life had shifted over the years?

Up until that point, I would have dismissed these stirrings. Traffic is a part of life, just suck it up. Other people have much worse commutes, so stop complaining about the thirty minutes in the car each way, which often ended up being two hours in the car on days we went to the yoga studio. Two hours in the car, even with listening to podcasts and doing other "productive" things, felt like a colossal waste of time.

Besides, my partner and I had been in our house for twenty years and had plans to retire in it. Moving to the other side of town would mean leaving the home we raised our kids in. We'd be starting over paying down a mortgage in order to have a house paid off before retirement.

But a little part of me asked, "What if...?"

Which made me realize that there were other things that I no longer loved about living in our home. The congestion of the space that had grown up over the years, the repairs that we were needing to make more and more around the house, and how much easier it is to access the things we love from the other side of town.

What would it hurt to look around to see what houses were available? Looking didn't commit us to buying anything.

But just acknowledging it as a possibility opened the floodgates. Before we knew it, we walked into a new home that was everything we were looking for, with an additional discount to buy right away. The equity that we had in our home that we sold allowed us to pay off all of our other debt – student loans, vehicle, credit cards – so that we were only paying for our new home and utilities, so dreaming paid off financially, too.

It almost felt like magical thinking, so I continued to test out the concept, and it continued to hold. Over the years, using the Perfect Day exercise gave me space to dream and give myself permission to develop hobbies, take time off without "cheating" and "checking in" on things, and travel farther than I could have ever thought possible while owning a business. Exploring the beauty of National Parks across the country, as well as getting to experience the cultures of Belize, Costa Rica, England, Spain, France, and Ireland, have breathed fresh life into my soul.

I used this concept to redefine the way I work. Instead of traditional weekly therapy sessions, I started thinking about the ways I work with clients that bring the most impactful results that actually aren't weekly, fifty-minute sessions. That dreaming resulted in the creation of two-day intensives that my clients have called "life-changing". These intensives give me the space to do the deep work with my clients and also do it at a pacing and with breaks that allow me to take good care of myself in the face of intense trauma work.

When the Perfect Day Goes Wrong

My Journey to My CVO Job Description

I've joked for YEARS about taking a sabbatical. Looking back, I think my heart knew what was coming, but my head was not hearing any of it until the spring of 2021, when my heart became more and more insistent.

There's something about the pacing of Spring that tends to leave me in a bit of a tailspin. Maybe it's that the freshness of the new year wears off. Maybe it's the ebbs and flows of the business. I've noticed it in the past, but by Spring 2021, I was really starting to FEEL how "in the weeds" I was.

For me, the imagery of "in the weeds" is the feeling of being just below the surface of the water. I'm trying desperately to get my head above the surface to take a gulp of fresh air, but the weeds at the bottom of the ocean are wrapped around my ankles, keeping me from doing so. They loosen occasionally, giving me just a moment with my head above water to take a gulp of air before being pulled down to the depths again.

I remember taking a break to walk on the beach in April, with nothing on the calendar to do and nothing to plan for at that moment, and thinking, "Finally, I can BREATHE!" And while this sounds like a good thing (and it was), it also sent me into a bit of a panic to realize that I wasn't remotely aware of how I *hadn't* been breathing for so long.

In years past, I was able to get away from this feeling with just a little break — a training, a workshop, a long weekend off — something that was just enough to take the edge off, to take that gulp of air. That wasn't going to work this time.

In May, I took a step out of the daily working *in* the business to take a business retreat to work *on* the business. The week away was the starting point of the unraveling. And by unraveling, I mean complete meltdown. Ever had one of those?

One of the challenges of being a business owner and entrepreneur is the blessing of growth. When I started my business, I had to do EVERYTHING because I was the only one to do ANYTHING. I was a solo practitioner: just me and the therapy dog.

As the business has grown, I've added more and more duties to my "owner/operator" role without even considering what I should be cutting back on — simply because it's what I've always done and because I didn't want to "burden" other people.

But I was doing "all the things," from seeing clients to supervising and leading our staff to policy making, visioning, networking, marketing, training, etc.

(I'm also weird in that I take satisfaction from seeing the mini-fridge filled so that our clients and therapists can grab a refreshing drink on their way into session! Of course, being stuck in the minutia doesn't help.)

No wonder it got to be too much! I was pulled in too many directions. (P.S., I also pretty much hate being limited by the time/space/energy continuum we humans must abide by).

The reality of this came crashing down on me as I got settled into this time away, pulled out my journal, and started thinking about my perfect day, only to realize that I was way off base in almost every way.

I cried during that retreat; *a lot*. It was scary to be *so* confronted with the truth that something had to change. I recognized that I would have to release control of some things, and that's scary, too. There was some grief around the reality that I'm not superhuman and able to do everything. (Hustle me was very caught up in her superhuman identity. Bless her.)

But I also had amazing support and got some clarity around the roles that I'm good at, the ones I most enjoy, and the ones that only I can fulfill. I got even more clarity around the fact that I couldn't keep doing what I was doing and expect different results (that classic definition of "insanity") and that trying to do so kept me from being the person I most wanted to be.

So Shamon (my business + life partner) and I sat down, got super clear about the things I should focus on, and wrote a job description for my new role as Chief Vision Officer.

I thought this new role would somehow magically solve all of my problems.

But, if I'm honest, there was STILL a part of me that thought I would keep doing things the same way, only with this new, fancy title (yes, I AM that stubborn).

What happened is that "hustle me" rebelled, and what I call an "existential apocalypse" occurred...

Hello, My Name is...?

As May 2021 was coming to a close, there was a little distance from my business retreat mini-unraveling and, if I'm honest with you (and myself), there was a part of me that thought that I could continue doing the same things, but cloaked under the label of my fancy new title of Chief Vision Officer.

Why am I surprised EVERY F'ING TIME that trying to do the same thing and expecting different results DOESN'T work?!?

Sigh.

Needless to say, that wasn't working.

So I started pulling back and eyeing September as an option to take a sabbatical. The idea was to be completely out of the office. Yay, a plan! But when I discussed my plan with my business coach, I was advised not to see clients from September through the rest of the year. I started to panic at that thought and literally thought I would pass out. They actually had to tell me to breathe; otherwise, I might have.

As a trauma therapist, my "productivity" and, therefore "worth" is calculated in the number of weekly therapy sessions on my calendar.

How many people I'm helping.

How many people are healing because of the work we do together.

Let's face it, "take the space to be creative" and "vision creator and protector" don't have the same immediate, jaw-dropping, inspiring outcomes as helping someone resolve their long-standing, debilitating trauma. Or helping a couple on the brink of divorce find connection, joy, and love again.

Somehow, I did not realize there would need to be some trade-off between the time seeing clients – what had become my identity – and this more "soft" work of my new title.

I did NOT agree to that when I accepted my new CVO position. This was bullsh!t

But it also resonated as being the right thing to do.

Sometimes the "right thing" is the hard thing. The uncomfortable thing. The unsettling thing.

When the Earth Shifts Beneath Your Feet

The first time I visited California, there was a little earthquake. I remember thinking, "Wait a minute, how is it possible that the earth is moving?" I lost my sense of direction and couldn't think clearly.

And as "trauma therapist" became less of a primary role, I felt that same sense of being unsteady on my feet. Again, I felt the familiar fog of grief – this time, grief around my identity.

Trauma therapy wasn't only what I did. It was who I was.

I bet this is similar for you. We focus so much of our identity on what we do, how we are "productive," and making a living and a name for ourselves. When we don't win a contract, our business is going poorly, or we recognize how unsustainable our current hustle pattern is, it can send us into this kind of tailspin.

Once again, I reached out for support from someone who had taken a similar shift away from primarily being a "trauma therapist" to their role of helping and making an impact more broadly. I asked for any guidance they could offer. Surprisingly, they said that they still consider themselves to be a trauma therapist – one who serves the world in a different way.

That was comforting because I can't see the world through a different lens. This allowed me to broaden my new/current "job description" and my heart's purpose into leaving a "Love Legacy"...

Leaving a LOVE LEGACY

I've been reading back through my journals from around the time I took a sabbatical in 2021 to remember when it was, exactly, that I met the phrase "Love Legacy," and I totally can't find it. Although I do index my journals so I can easily go back and find important information, the phrase never stood out as something to take special note of. Instead, it always felt very natural. "Of course!" my heart said when I landed on it.

Love Legacy is a blend of all of my parts–a combination of the doing and being. Years ago, my business coach,Calibrate Your Year with Kelly Higdon, commented that I need to always have a "bigger project" that I'm working on that keeps me out of the weeds of my daily grind.

She was completely right about that, and Love Legacy helps me to balance the micro and the macro. It incorporates every job description and also stands on its own.

Love Legacy =

- Helping people heal— emotionally, spiritually, mentally, relationally.
- Helping others know that they're not alone in their struggle. To be human is to struggle. We're in the mess of life together.
- Helping people connect to themselves and others.
- To be a leader in the mental health field, highlighting quality mental health in ways that don't suck the life out of therapists.
- Living counter-culturally in ways that honor my body, mind, and soul and don't blindly adhere to broken societal systems.
- Making a difference.
- Helping others know that they are loved and are worthy of love.
- To be a part of something bigger than myself.
- Loving and being loved by my tribe.

My Soul Sabbatical gave me time and space to get clear about these things. Through meditation, journaling, reading, moving my body through yoga, hiking, Peloton rides, and listening to music, I asked myself some really important questions that I keep coming back to over and over...

- Why am I doing what I'm doing? What is mine to do at this moment?
- What if the legacy is bigger than I could ever imagine, but I can only see what's right in front of me in the box I'm living in? I am capable of things I haven't even thought of yet.
- What if winning means keeping my peace and taking my time?
- Why do I insult my potential with doubt?

- What would my life look like if I lived fully into my heart and instinct? They have a pretty good track record for guiding me up to this point.
- What if the thing that I've always thought was my kryptonite is actually my superpower?
- What if I'm worth doing something hard for?
- What if I gave myself the gold star I look to others for?
- What if I CAN?

And, of course, I geeked out when I was creating my vision board for 2022 and came across the phrase:

Leave a Legacy of Love

God conspires to speak directly to our hearts. We have to get still to listen.

Part of my commitment to living and leaving a Love Legacy, and what helps to guide me when crafting my Perfect Day, is to ask myself regularly…

What do I need?

What do I need to feed my soul? To hear my heart's dreams? To allow those dreams to lead me to living a Love Legacy. To open myself to things I never imagined myself doing?

For too many years, I turned the sound off on my needs. Honestly, that's still the path of least resistance for me, but I'm committed to the practice of doing something different. So I remind myself to pay attention to my wisdom.

Lately, I've been noticing my internal chatter questioning whether it's all worth it, if I'm actually up for the challenge, or if I can face yet another hard thing.

I'm learning that, instead of my typical freeze response, I can choose other options.

Soul Sabbatical

Living into your dreams is far from a "one and done" pause for a moment of reflection. It's a practice for the long haul—something to incorporate into the remainder of our lives. It takes endurance.

It makes me think of my endurance rides on my Peloton. The longest one I've done is 90 minutes. That's a long time on a bike seat. It's a long time to move my legs. But as long as it is for my rear and my legs, it's an even longer time mentally.

Endurance rides don't mean crushing effort. They mean pedaling through the long haul. This is the perfect metaphor for my life right now. Nothing particularly effortful or devastating is happening. Just life. And it feels like there's no letting up.

And this feels like it's squeezing any space for my heart.

One of my favorite endurance rides is a good combination of inspiring music and encouraging words. This is one of my favorite instructors, and I knew this ride would offer an opportunity to be a moving meditation.

Then I got halfway through the ride. And I was tired. The chatter in my head started.

"Is it really worth it?"

"What if this is a waste of time?"

"There are so many more productive things you could do in ninety minutes."

But it was met by the message from the instructor and the music.

What if you take one more step forward?

What if you proved to yourself that you will show up for yourself?

What if you can surprise yourself?

And I did.

And I want to remind you...

You're capable of taking one step forward. It doesn't have to be effortful. In fact, the dreaming itself is the opposite of effort.

You can surprise yourself.

One step at a time; one pedal stroke at a time; one moment at a time, following your heart.

You can live into your biggest dreams and desires. The biggest meaning in your life that you don't even know is there... yet.

What do you need right now so that you can open up to your heart and your dreams?

Your Heart is Invited

Settle into a quiet space and take a few deep breaths. Now picture what a Perfect Day would look like for you in as much detail as possible.

What time do you wake up? Alarm or no alarm?

What's the first thing you do when you get out of bed?

What's your morning routine?

What does the flow of your day look like? How does it feel?

What are you eating during the day?

How are you dressed?

Who are you spending time with?

What are you spending your time doing?

What rituals are part of your day?

What do you spend your free time doing?

What are you reading, watching, making, saying, and dreaming of?

If you'd like, write down what this Perfect Day looks like.

Then take a look at one thing you can do – an action you can take, small or large – to move you toward the reality of that day.

Maybe you go to bed earlier. Wake up later. Have time in the morning for a cup of coffee and meditation before you start your day. Maybe you look at houses across town. Or update your resume. Or start a new class.

Yes, you can. :)

Chapter 5
Exquisite Kindness

"Kindness is not an afterthought to our work. It is the driving power for everything we do. It is the lens we view every challenge through. To me, almost every problem you can think of can be solved with kindness."

— Lady Gaga

We live in a world that is becoming increasingly unkind. The anonymity of social media can mean that we encounter cruelty throughout each day. Words can and do hurt.

But maybe you learned of cruelty much earlier in your life. Perhaps, for you, it looked like the biting criticism of a parent, and those words continue to play on an endless sound loop in your mind.

For many of us, it's the condemning, shaming messages from whatever organized religion we were exposed to; the fear of facing the wrath of an angry god.

Regardless of where we first experienced cruelty, the result is the same... we shut down our hearts. Out of protection. Out of preservation. Out of survival.

But it's time for kindness to make a comeback.

Exquisite Kindness from Others

Just in case you've missed it, I want to be explicitly clear here. A Soul Sabbatical does not happen in isolation. It simply can't.

In fact, part of the Soul Sabbatical is getting super clear about your people. Your support system. Your cheer squad. Your tribe.

The problem is that our society is the most superficially connected but also the most lonely it's ever been.

With social media, our contacts are a mile wide and an inch deep. We can even find ourselves making big life decisions or not based on feedback from our connections on Facebook, Instagram, and Twitter.

In case you haven't realized it yet, this isn't working for any of us. These platforms can be a place of profound unkindness. Our friends and followers there are swimming in the same waters that we've been in, but many haven't yet recognized that they want a different way of living. They don't understand that we're attempting to play by a different set of rules. So focusing our attention here will keep us stuck in the same old box.

I know that playing the social media comparison game and being shut down when I questioned the status quo or posed doing things differently kept me stifled for way too long. I finally stopped beating my head against the social media wall and gave myself some distance from it. I still use social media, but it's no longer a news source for me – about the world or my value and worth based on how many likes and comments I get.

Let's also be clear about the number of people who will journey with you into your Soul Sabbatical. In a world where we're looking to add followers and fans, and friends, the answer might surprise you:

Not many.

My general rule of thumb is to take a piece of paper and draw a one-inch square. The number of people who should journey with you into your Soul Sabbatical should fit in that box. Not tens or hundreds or thousands.

Just two to five, if that.

Soul Sabbatical

These are people who are not in your life because of what you do or how you can benefit them, or how flashy your life is from the outside, but because they see all of your parts and love you, not in spite of your imperfections, but through them and because of them.

These are the people who you would call in the middle of the night if you were in trouble, the ones who have a history of staying by your side when life gets messy. You get excited when you're with them. They fill you rather than deplete your energy. You have the fun, as well as the hard conversations with each other. These are not just "yes" people who rubber stamp what you bring to them. They're just as likely to hold you accountable as they are to cheer you on. They ask the hard questions, challenge you, and let you know if they're worried that you're way off path, but do it with kindness. They ooze curiosity over judgment, and you can feel this tangibly when you're with them. You don't need to explain yourself or justify who you are because they take the time to know and understand you.

After more than three decades together, my husband falls into this category.

As I got a better understanding of what was going on for me while I worked through the inconsistencies of my perfect day and asking my heart what it needed, I got a better understanding of the other people who would go on the journey with me.

It started with the people that were at the business retreat with me – a small group of us who had known each other through several years of working with the same business coaches. I already knew from our history together that we were like-minded, and I quickly found out that we were similarly like-hearted.

During the week we spent together, I felt like the rug had been pulled out from under me. My head swam, and my heart burst wide open. I felt confused and exposed, and at the same time, I felt so very seen and held by them.

Do you know this feeling? I both wouldn't wish it on anyone and hope that everyone in the world could experience it.

Vulnerability is uncertainty, risk, and emotional exposure. Compassion is suffering together. Not once during that week did I feel alone. There were countless hours of conversation during work sessions, over meals, and while hiking that helped me better understand the magnitude of what I was experiencing. Together, we shared many "me too" and "you're not alone" conversations, which helped combat my thoughts that I was being ridiculous. That I was making a big deal out of nothing. Or, one of the things I fear the most – being seen as being too needy.

This small group of people was (and remains) my cheer squad, my sounding board, and my (loving) accountability team. In fact, they cheered me on as I wrote this book. A funny thing happens when you're in community. As one person is brave enough to be vulnerable and try something different, it gives others permission to do so, as well. Other people went on a sabbatical journey that I got to support them on. More and more of our conversations with one another have shifted toward what our hearts desire, and when we get together from across the country, we spend our time, energy, and resources doing the things that delight our hearts. When I see messages from them, my heart sings. I would not be the person that I am today without these people.

Getting Clear About Who's Not On the List:

I've also learned along the way about the people who have not earned the right to be part of your support circle. If you think of concentric circles, the ones in the innermost circle are the ones we've discussed above.

The people on the next tier are the most challenging to navigate, I think. They are people who are important to you – possibly family members or friends, people that you connect with regularly. But they don't "get it." And you really want them to "get it." Still, no matter how much you try, they're not willing or able to perspective-take. Although they may be your go-to for other things – parenting, gardening, relationships, how to go about learning your new hobby – your heart is not completely safe with them in this area.

This does not make them bad people. But it does bring up a lot of grief when you thought you'd get support from them and don't. They're still close enough to have an understanding that you're doing something different, but you might not share the how and why behind it.

I learned to get clear about what I felt comfortable communicating to these people and what didn't feel safe and to be very direct about communicating that I was taking time away from the office and typical duties for a sabbatical. If they asked probing questions, I would give a general response about needing time off and then change the topic.

Afterward, I would acknowledge how I wished the conversation with that person could be different instead of burying that feeling of grief. Oh, how I've learned to be with my grief! I told myself that it was understandable to be sad that I had hoped that this person would be someone that I could share with and get support from when, in reality, they could not or would not be that person for me. But, I would also remind myself that I wasn't doing anything "wrong" just because someone couldn't understand (or agree with) why I was doing something.

I also reminded myself of this when interacting with people on the outer tier of my circle. I was very intentional about what, if anything, I said on broader platforms, such as social media. The process was too tender for me to open my heart to unkind comments from people who didn't have an understanding of my truth nor cared to understand. Just because you know me doesn't mean that you have access to the most sacred parts of me. So having any kind of conversation with the nay-sayers was a hard "no" for me.

Do some of your people come to mind when I talk about the inner circle? What are your criteria for these people? Who's on the "no" list? Take some time to fill in those circles. Then take even more time to fill in the middle tier. Go slowly, and notice how your body responds to these names. Tension in your muscles, an "ick" feeling in your stomach, and a tightness in your throat are all good indicators that you might need more space from this person. Also, know that people can move between circles depending on the situation, their behavior, the particular season of life, and their relationship with one another. Stay curious with yourself.

The Kindness of What is Bigger Than You

"I think the most important question facing humanity is, 'Is the universe a friendly place?' This is the first and most basic question all people must answer for themselves."

— Albert Einstein

I grew up in a very conservative household. We went to church whenever the doors were open. Church gave me a sense of safety and belonging when things were turbulent and chaotic at home. Church gave me a solid foundation of the head truths of my faith. Church gave me the ability to cite Scripture, chapter and verse. At church, I found moments of peace, especially through song, whether during the formal service, choir practice and presentations, or playing handbells.

But church also taught me to be a "good girl" – one that doesn't question anything. Church set the standard of giving of myself above and beyond what is good or healthy for me AT ALL TIMES, to work sacrificially always. Period. It caused me to experience God as a judge on high, not really interested in the details of my life (I mean, the Bible says that he knows the number of hairs on my head, but does he *really* care when he's got so many more important things to do?). That I would be zapped for the slightest misstep.

It took me years to realize how the church and organized religion in general – not just Judeo-Christian traditions – has components of being steeped in patriarchy, hyper-capitalism, power, and control. And while I know this is not true across all congregations, the combination of these things made me think of God/the universe as scary. And, for the record, I also grew up believing that other people were out to cause you harm and should not be trusted and that I could not trust myself. As a result, I lived in a constant state of fear and tried to make myself - physically and emotionally - as small as possible. Any attention, after all, could possibly be not just negative but an experience of brute force.

This started shifting several years ago when, to be quite honest, I found myself depressed and on a therapist's couch because of the unrealistic weight I was trying to carry to please God and all of the people around me. I slowly started to question the voice of God I had playing in my head– the voice that was chronically harsh, critical, demanding, and angry. Slowly, this voice started sounding not quite as harsh and judgemental as it had in the past.

Then, there was a moment when I was sitting on a beach in Kauai with my husband, where we had taken a trip for our 10th wedding anniversary. As I took in the beauty of the Napali Coast, I internally "heard" the voice that I have experienced as loving God saying, "I put those mountains there for you."

Wait. What?

I remember thinking how grandiose an idea that was. As if the mountains and the land had nothing to do with the native people who inhabited it.

And a heartbeat later, my husband rolled over on the sand and lazily said to me, "God put those mountains there for us." My heart was shaken to the core. And from that moment on, I've been listening for the voice of the exquisite kindness of God.

I find it in the quiet depth of my soul, along with my wisdom and my strength. Sometimes it comes to me as I'm driving and listening to the radio when that one perfect song plays.

Soul Sabbatical

Sometimes it comes to me as I sit on the beach or have my feet on a mountain trail. When I am still and listen.

It comes with a tender gaze of absolute love and acceptance, with goodness and kindness, even through war and racial injustice, and pandemics. It's an understanding in my depth that I'm connected to a sense of peace and purpose, something bigger than myself that binds me to all humanity. It comes with a knowing that whatever comes, I am held. And in this being held, a "knowing" about the things that I'm meant to do, like take a sabbatical or work remotely for a month or write a book. That these things might not be what I expected or look the way I think they should, but they will work out. This "knowing" is based on a track record that everything that has come before, as hard as it sometimes is, always does.

I often make a distinction between organized religion and this journey of spirituality. I haven't completely left my faith or the church, but I do engage with it differently so that I can more fully bask in the presence of an exquisitely kind God. This, in turn, makes me more kind.

Finding Kindness Within

If you're like me and the rest of humanity, you have a pretty vocal, inner itty bitty shitty committee. We each come by our committee honestly– it's often the internalized voice of a childhood caregiver, coach, teacher, or a chorus of several critical voices. It makes total sense because that's the way we're conditioned; we are pushed to become "better" with harshness and often even shame. And while harshness is jarring and an affront to the senses, shame hits us at the core of who we are as human beings and sends the message that the thing that we're doing wrong impacts our worthiness of love and belonging.

Because our brains are assessing the environment for danger four times per second and naturally hone in on anything negative, the message that we internalize is "get it together, or you might not make it here." Not only is what you're doing wrong or bad or not good enough, but YOU YOURSELF are also wrong, bad, and not good enough. And because our brain's job is to protect us from danger and being outcast, it internalizes this message even if these are not the words that were explicitly said to you.

So, in order to beat everyone else to the punch, we learn to be harsh and shaming to ourselves.

And, every time we do so, our heart withers a bit more and more. Because the truth is:

There is no positive change in the vibration of shame.

It doesn't work. Oh, it might SEEM like it works, in the moment. You get your act together. Get shit done. Pull yourself up by your bootstraps. Make things right. BUT IT COMES AT A COST. And the cost is increased anxiety, depression, eating disorders, risky/self-harm behaviors, bullying, violence, isolation, and so much more.

But because shame, harshness, criticism, condemnation, and unkindness are the waters we swim in, we can't even fathom that there might be another way.

Is That Even ALLOWED?

A longtime friend and I were Army Brats who met on a military base in Germany when we were in middle school. One of the first conversations we had was around our disbelief that NOT EVERYONE GOES TO COLLEGE! We had both experienced the expectation that we would go to college as the norm and never thought to question it. We thought this rule was universal and didn't even know there were any other options.

I remember having a similar feeling when I heard the phrase "self-compassion." Actually, to be quite honest, I initially thought the idea was dumb, woo-woo, and unrealistic. But when God wants me to pay attention to something, he bombards me with the topic from several different directions, and before I knew it, I was hearing about self-compassion everywhere. Then I realized, WAIT A MINUTE!!! There's actual RESEARCH about the benefits of a self-compassion practice. At the time, I was definitely in more of a headspace than a heart space, so the word RESEARCH gave the concept some legitimacy and gave my head "permission" to explore it.

But it's far from a head practice. And it's been a complete game changer for me.

Three Steps of Self-Compassion

1. Pay Attention

The first step in a practice of self-compassion is to recognize we're in a struggle. That we're hurt and we're suffering. Ouch.

The problem is that we've learned to push pain – whether it's physical pain, emotional pain, mental pain, relational pain, or spiritual pain – down, down, down. We don't know how to deal with it, and we don't want to deal with it. If we sweep it under the rug and don't acknowledge it, surely it will go away, right?

We don't realize that when we stockpile the pain, push it down, and add more and more and more on top of it, it builds and builds and builds. Before we know it, it's like a volcano erupting hot lava all over us and everyone around us, and it becomes overwhelming.

Bringing mindfulness to the difficult things that would typically invite your internal critic to the table means that you acknowledge the struggle without under-identifying with it (building a brick wall around it) and without over-identifying with it (being lost in the muck and the mire of the swampland with no way out). It's reminding ourselves that this difficult thing is not going to last forever, and we don't need to get caught up in the story that we tell ourselves about it (or, heaven forbid, what your itty bitty shitty committee is telling you will happen), but in THIS MOMENT, life is hard.

I remember coming to understand this overall concept of mindfulness during a yoga class when I was a beginning yogi. I love my yoga practice, and part of what I love about it is the opportunity to bring this mindfulness piece into my practice. I used to try to plow through any pose that became difficult, as if pressing harder into it would actually achieve the desired pose.

One day, I was beating myself up because my pigeon pose didn't look like the instructor's pigeon pose. I held my breath and tried to force myself deeper into it, but my body just wouldn't bend in that way.

Frustrated, I gave up.

I pulled back out of the pose just until the point where I first started to notice the tension. Then, instead of trying to push past it, I stayed there. And breathed. And thought, "Man, I wish I could go deeper. And this is the truth of where I'm at at this moment."

And, in that moment, I got a sense of what it meant to be mindful. Struggles come and go. Emotions come and go. Flexibility comes and goes. I can learn to be present to what is.

Now, when I experience the pain of comparison, grief, or conflict with my partner, I pay attention. I notice the ouch instead of pushing it down. I bring myself to the middle ground of not choosing to stay in the pain and also not choosing to amplify it. I remind myself that this is what is true right here, right now. It won't last forever. And it becomes more manageable. Most importantly, I don't act out on it like I do when I try to ignore it.

2. You're Not Alone

The second step to self-compassion is to recognize that *you are not alone in your suffering*. When we're in shame, especially, we tend to feel that we're the only one in the world who is broken enough, flawed enough, damaged enough, dumb enough, ugly enough (I could go on and on, but you get the picture, right?) to have the hard thing happen to us. We forget that hard things are part of the human condition. None of us are exempt. We all suffer. My topic of suffering might be slightly different from your topic, my flavor different from your flavor, but we all experience struggle, loss, failure… the whole array of painful experiences.

And because of the glorification of rugged individualism in our society, we don't realize that we were never meant to carry these burdens alone. We hide behind the facade of having it all together, perfectionism, unflappable strength, and calm in the midst of disaster, forgetting the healing behind two of the most powerful words in the English language:

Me too.

You are not alone.

The simple act of saying this to myself when I'm feeling pain – reminding myself that I'm not the only person grieving, not the only person who's been hurt by someone I love, not the only person angry at injustice – helps me to remind myself that I'm not bad or wrong for feeling the way I do. It also reminds me that I don't have to shoulder the pain alone. Others understand.

3. Just Be Nice

I think one of the most life-changing and most difficult parts of a self-compassion practice is talking kindly to yourself, the way that you would to a good friend, a child, or a beloved pet.

The definition of compassion is the desire to alleviate suffering.

Does what you're saying to yourself align with that concept?

For most of us, the answer to that is "no." Self-compassion starts with non-violence between your ears. At the very least, don't call yourself names. Truly, we talk to ourselves in ways that we would never dare talk to anyone else!

So if talking kindly to yourself is like trying to speak a foreign language, start with how you would talk to someone you care deeply about when they're in pain. Now say that thing to yourself.

Warning: This will feel so uncomfortable at first– it feels scripted, dumb, or weird, but weird is good. Because you're used to the slime that you've been swimming in, if you're having a hard time, here are some phrases to try out.

I'm here.

You're not alone.

I've got your back, sweetheart.

You did your best.

It's not your fault.

Now you know what you can do differently next time.

It's ok to rest.

Nobody is perfect.

Thank you for trying so hard.

I LOVE YOU.

Find words and phrases that resonate with you. Ones that move your heart, even if they seem corny to critical-you. I promise the more you do this, the less awkward it will start to feel, and the more you'll see the benefits.

Kind Touch

To continue with the "this is really weird, are you sure about this?" vein, let's add kind self-touch to the practice. As mammals, we are wired for touch. We absolutely have to have it (remember the failure to thrive babies in the orphanages in Russia?). We need it from other people. And we need it from ourselves.

Adding a kind touch to our kind words magnifies the outcome. It allows the experience to imbed itself into our minds, hearts, and bodies. But what, exactly, is kind touch? Let's try these out (try reading through all of these and then practice them one by one. Put the book down, lower your eye gaze, or close your eyes, and really feel your body):

> **Heart.** Place one or both hands on your heart. Feel the warmth and the weight of your hands on your chest. Feel your heart beating. Do this for several breaths.

> **Gut.** We hold a lot of emotions in our belly/gut area, so place one or two hands on your abdomen and notice the

warmth and weight of your hands there. Allow your breath to drop from your chest into this belly area, and notice the rise and fall of your abdomen as you do this. You might notice a bit of relaxation with each breath. Note that, in our super-body shaming culture, focusing your attention on your belly can be especially challenging. It can be even more challenging to allow your belly to relax, expand, and take up space. It's often true that the thing we most dislike is the thing we need the most, so check in with yourself to see if this is true for you – if you have extra shame around the size and shape of your body. Allow yourself a gentle touch on your belly, sending the slightest iota of love in that direction, then explore other body parts. But keep returning to this one until it starts feeling a bit more comfortable.

Heart and Gut. Place one hand on your heart and one hand on your abdomen. Notice the weight and warmth at each location on your body. Follow your breath from your nose/mouth to your chest to your belly and notice the rise and fall of your belly and your chest. Take several breaths here.

Hands. Hold your own hand. Notice your own supportive presence here. Take several breaths. (I love this one because you can do it inconspicuously anywhere!!)

Hug. Give yourself a big hug. Breathe in the warmth, support, and feeling of security across your chest and shoulders.

Cheeks. Place one hand on each of your cheeks and the

side of your face, like you're holding the face of a young child. Notice the sensations in your body as you do so.

Why Do This?

Did you follow along in these exercises? If so, thanks for giving it a try! If you're leary, I get it. It's weird. It's corny. It feels self-indulgent.

But as the trauma therapist and brain geek that I am, let me share with you what's happening in your brain when you practice self-compassion.

You're moving your brain out of that lizard fight, flight, freeze response to shame into your prefrontal cortex, thinking brain. It's actually a healthier way of motivating yourself (think of the difference between a harsh coach and one who is encouraging – which one do you work harder for?). And the research shows many other benefits, such as improving self-esteem and body image, decreasing anxiety and depression, bettering relationships and physical health, boosting happiness and emotional intelligence, and so much more.

And personally, I've found that this practice has helped me to hold onto my values and integrity to the person I want to be during difficult times. And it carried me through the uncertainty leading up to and during my sabbatical.

Give it a Try

So go back to the physical touch that resonated the most with you – hand on heart, hands on belly, hand on heart and belly, holding your own hand, hugging yourself, holding your hands on your cheeks.

Take a deep breath and silently say the phrases that resonate the most with you to yourself. The ones of kindness and support.

Honor your pain, your interests, and your heart with kindness. Because there's nothing that harshness can do that loving kindness can't do better.

May you be safe. May you be happy. May you be healthy. May you live with ease.

Fierce Self Compassion

There's a tender, nurturing energy to the practice of self-compassion that we explored above. A being held with gentle love. But sometimes, what we need is the fierce energy of a protective mama bear.

Sometimes the next best thing that you can do for yourself, the ultimate in "self-care", is the hard thing.

Sometimes it's starting a yoga practice, choosing fruit over processed food, going to bed earlier, or trying meditation (again).

Getting off the phone and connecting IRL.

Sometimes it's having the vulnerable conversation.

Speaking kindly to yourself even as your inner critic is screaming its head off. (You don't get control this time, shame).

Putting the boundary in place. Sticking to the boundary.

Honoring the boundary placed before you.

Being present to your grief instead of stuffing it down.

Attending your first AA meeting.

Attending your 100th AA meeting.

Being willing to step away from the toxic work environment that is literally killing you.

Picking up the phone to schedule your first therapy appointment.

There will be moments where you feel silly, scared, or terrified, or feel like you simply won't survive the hard thing.

That's normal.

It means you're doing something very brave.

Fierce self-compassion looks like the victory stance, with your arms held overhead in a wide V. It's an immovable posture of standing with your feet planted firmly on the floor and your hands on your hips, holding your ground. It's a no-nonsense position of holding your hand out at the end of an outstretched arm, indicating a boundary that says "STOP."

It sounds like:

- I am strong.
- I can do hard things.
- I deserve this.
- I can be afraid and brave at the same time.

Try these on. How do they feel?

Whatever your hard thing is today — remember that you can do it. And you've got me over here, cheering you on.

Meeting Your Heart with Exquisite Kindness

I used to joke that I could never trust someone who couldn't stay on their mat through savasana, the "corpse pose" of stillness and silence at the end of a yoga class, but I get it. It's scary to be with ourselves when things get quiet and our shadow parts come to the surface. When you're terrified of who you think you are.

I hear from women regularly that they love the idea of taking a sabbatical but are terrified of what might come bubbling up when they slow down.

The only way to our hearts is through the shadowy darkness and out of the waters we've been swimming in. Through the months leading up to my sabbatical and during the weeks I spent with myself during it, these forms of exquisite kindness held in ways that I could have never anticipated, but I'm so thankful for.

Your heart is invited to kindness. It's surprisingly powerful.

Your Heart is Invited

How can we come to know this Exquisite Kindness so that we can live from its depths?

This kind of kindness, this sort of love, cannot be fully understood by the mind. It has to be experienced. This practice is an invitation to encounter your heart and its exquisite kindness and to be able to replicate this process at any time. This practice is an invitation to encounter love in its very physical and very connective form.

Place the palm of one hand on your heart. Feel your heart beating in your chest, through your chest, into the palm of your hand. Let the rhythm of your heart bring you into this present moment and into an awareness of the sufficiency of this very moment. One beat after the next is a reminder that, in this very moment, you have all that you need. You ARE all that you need.

Bring to your mind a loved one, a beloved pet, a special place, or anything else that brings you great delight and a feeling of love. Let the joy bring a smile to your face. This joyful moment is cemented in your being. It's an undeniably, spontaneous, precious experience.

Bring this beloved being or thing from your mind and down to your heart center. Feel it land just under your palm. Allow your mind and heart to relax, and feel your heart space open up with warmth and love for this person or thing. Smile.

Now, gently place a challenging person or situation in your wide-open heart space. This challenging person might even be your own critical voice to yourself. The challenge might be other parts of yourself that you don't like. Continue to smile as you hold this challenging person in the very center of your heart.

Allow the difficult person or situation to be swallowed by the warmth of your heart. Ask your heart's wisdom and love to take over. Rest for a moment in this LOVE that loves you and the other, and wants to transform all into its loving image. Smile.

When you're ready, release the images. Release the thoughts. Release the practice. Open your eyes, knowing that you carry your heart forward with you and can access this anytime.

Chapter 6
Stuck Between the World You Need to Release and the World You're Afraid to Enter

Come to the edge

I first had the opportunity to paddle board in 2017 at a therapist retreat. I remember watching the other conference attendees paddling across Lake Michigan and noticed something stirring in me.

"That looks amazing. So peaceful and zen. Like you're one with the water."

But I never got on a paddle board on that trip. Most of that had to do with endless brain chatter that was on loop in my head: I had never done it before. I'm not the kind of person who does water activities. I'm not in good enough shape to stand on a board and paddle. What if I can't do it?

What if I fall off?

But even though I never got on a paddle board that trip, I thought about it afterward. Like, I thought about it A LOT. Almost obsessively.

Did you know that research shows that people's biggest regrets when they come to the end of their lives are the things they DIDN'T do?

Not the things they tried to do and failed.

Not the things they struggled with.

Not the things they did imperfectly.

Not the things they were afraid to do but did anyway (often with shaky knees!).

When reviewing their life, people most regret the things they didn't do.

When I had the opportunity to try paddle boarding again in 2018, I had the same worries.

What if I fall off the board?

But I also remembered the regret of not giving it a try.

And I finally told myself, "Well, if I fall off the board, I'll get wet. Getting wet is not the end of the world. Then I can get back on the board and give it another try."

Humans are creatures of habit- even when the habit doesn't serve us. We prefer homeostasis – the status quo. We tend not to like change and will usually choose the evil we know over the uncertainty of what we don't know.

It's why we stay in the same town or the same career or the same relationship or the same limiting beliefs, or the same whatever, even though it's suffocating us.

Homeless Under a Bridge

Oftentimes we do this because, in our brain's attempt to protect us, it gives us every worst-case scenario on the planet in full and vivid detail.

And when your brain does this, it can't tell the difference between this made-up story and reality. So to your brain, it's the same...damn...thing.

Then, if you're like me, you have lived experiences that compound the brain's innate way of operating. I am a self-proclaimed Enneagram 6. The Enneagram is a system of describing personality types, honing in on a person's core motivations and fears. So this means that, basically, I see danger in everything. It's part of my personality. It's part of my history. Because fear and danger are the lenses I instinctively see the world through, I have to work extra hard to adjust this lens. Otherwise, I'd never leave the house or try anything new.

Soul Sabbatical

I have a game I've learned to play with myself when my brain starts this kind of catastrophizing that I call "Homeless Under a Bridge" because my brain's worst-case outcome is usually some version of this concern. I sense danger, and before I know it, I'm living in a bad country song where I've lost my house, dog, and my love.

Shifting that to something different starts with me recognizing the signs that it's happening. My body has ways of cueing me in that things are beginning to spiral, like how I'm clenching my jaw, bracing my shoulders, and barely breathing. I notice that my brain is on an endless loop.

In the past, this was my cue to press in harder, problem-solve, or please people. My cue to fix, to hustle harder. I lean hard into over-functioning, believing that if I think really hard and try really hard, I can fix it.

Until I realized that this didn't fix anything; in fact, it usually made things worse and definitely left me exhausted.

Now, I pause.

I breathe.

I place a hand on my heart. I talk to myself. Yes, it sounds weird, but the truth is that we all do it. It's just that many of us aren't aware that we do it. And the words we say to ourselves are usually critical and continue to amplify the problem.

So instead, I allow the wise part of me – the part that knows that I have the capacity to get through things – to talk to the part of me that's scared. The part of me that's panicked. The part of me that's freaking out.

I say to myself, "Oh, my, this feels so big and scary. It's ok to feel afraid. I'm here with you. Let's talk through this together...

What, exactly, would have to happen for you actually to end up homeless under a bridge?"

Then, the wise part of me walks the scared part through the steps:

First, I'd have to shut down my business completely.

Go through all savings.

Through every investment.

Foreclose on the house.

Lose the camper.

Be mentally incapacitated to the point where I couldn't make decisions to pivot in another direction along the way.

AND

Lose all of the people in my life who would never actually allow me to live homeless under a bridge without intervening to help.

Ok, then. That gives a different perspective. And when my brain starts revving up again, I gently remind that fight/flight/freeze lizard part of my brain that it's ok to be uncomfortable about doing something different, but it no longer gets to drive the bus. Then I invite my wise self and my heart to take the wheel.

It Starts Small

Wait a minute. How did we get from a paddle board to Homeless Under a Bridge?

Playing the Homeless Under the Bridge game takes some practice. I didn't get good at playing the Homeless Under the Bridge game right away. Like anything important, it's taken lots of reps. Your version of Homeless Under the Bridge will take lots of practice too.

Remember that the whole purpose of playing this game is to reality-check the catastrophic story your brain is making up about a situation. To actively remember that just because your brain thinks a thought doesn't make it true. But sometimes, facing down what our brain is sensing as a big threat, like taking a Soul Sabbatical, can feel overwhelming. There are too many big, bad things that could go wrong.

It's been helpful for me to start with a smaller scenario with less dire consequences, like the paddle board. For example, if I fall off of a paddleboard, I might get wet. And while I don't love to get wet, I can recognize that it's not the end of the world to be a little wet and uncomfortable for a while once I've climbed back on the paddleboard and returned to shore.

I might be afraid that I'll have a hard time getting back on the board if I fall off, so I can start in more shallow waters, where it's easier to get on and off the board. I can practice getting on and off the board from different angles, leading with varying body parts, to find out if it feels easier to pull myself forward onto the board from its back or sit on it from its side.

This helps me to recognize and remember that there are many different ways for me to problem-solve – well beyond the options that my frightened brain gives me at the beginning of thinking about the scary thing. As a result, I won't be stuck treading water for the rest of my life! (Note: in the moment, it sure FEELS like the hard thing will last forever until I remind myself that nothing is truly forever.)

When I slow down and break down all of my fears about getting on the paddle board, I realize how much of my fear of falling off the paddle board is based on me being embarrassed to be seen falling off of a paddle board. Then I get to decide how important it is to me if others see this. I get to edit the story that I'm making up about what they're thinking when they see me. I can assume that they are judging me, or I can assume that they think it's cool that I'm giving it a try. Or, I can decide that it doesn't matter what they're thinking, that what they're thinking about me has no bearing on my life, that it's none of my business, and get on the damn board.

It might sound silly that I've given this much thought and attention to something like paddle boarding, but again, practicing using this tool in the laboratory with these smaller things over time serves a purpose when the stakes are higher.

On to Bigger Things

When I think about doing something as big as going on an extended sabbatical, the outcome feels much riskier. But breaking down the many paddleboard-level fears has helped me to develop a well-worn path to talk myself down from catastrophe regarding these bigger things.

And sometimes I have to break down the bigger changes, like a Sabbatical, into smaller, more manageable ones. For example, when I was first considering taking a sabbatical, I realized that I would be chunking out the whole process of a sabbatical into pieces that included being away from home for a week, out of the office for a month, and not seeing clients for three months, because all of those things together was a way too big Homeless Under a Bridge scenario.

So I started breaking each of these down, beginning with the easiest–the first week of my sabbatical, when I decided to go on a hiking trip. Being away from home, hiking for a week felt like pretty low stakes that I could practice the process. I've been away on a trip plenty of times before (just not in conjunction with being out of the office for a month!), and I could see that booking a flight and hotel was doable for me to start slowly creating momentum.

Not seeing clients for several months was the next-easiest thing to work through, so I broke that down into steps – talking to my clients about being out of the office and finding referrals for them. It surprised me that this brought up some purpose and identity questions for me, so I slowed the process down and got curious about those questions. I got curious about what it meant for me to identify as a trauma therapist, as well as what was left of me and how I identified myself when I was not actively doing that thing. It was a good reminder that I'm more than the sum of what I do. I learned that monitoring the speed of the Homeless Under the Bridge process is important for me to keep making slow but steady progress instead of getting overwhelmed and shutting down.

Being completely removed from all aspects of running my business was, by far, the greatest challenge, mostly because I was over-involved in every single aspect– not just in policy, procedure, supervising, leading, and managing the team, but also where we stocked the toilet paper and making runs to the store for bottled water and other supplies.

As most over-functioners can identify with, I was terrified that the whole business would fall apart if I stepped away. The gift of the sabbatical is that I was forced to play the Homeless Under a Bridge game with each of my roles within the business. What was I most afraid was going to happen for our students if I wasn't around to supervise them? They wouldn't automatically become rotten therapists without my input. In fact, my being gone would give them the gift of learning from the other therapists on our team.

I played the Homeless Under a Bridge game countless times before and during my sabbatical, with every scenario I could dream up. Then I reminded myself over and over again...It's going to be ok. It's going to be ok. I knew that, if I needed to, I could step right back into things. But I also reminded myself of the cost of doing that. The cost of things staying the same. The cost of doing the same thing over and over again and expecting different results. Every time I wanted to jump back into the same old, same old, I had to very intentionally slow down, breathe, talk myself through it, and do something to move my body in order to move out some of the anxious energy that had risen in my body.

What Will People Think?

I also recognized how much other people's opinions played into releasing the world of over-functioning and hustle and entering into the peace and joy of living a soul sabbatical.

As an Enneagram 6 Type, loyalty is important to me, greatly impacting my sense of belonging. I realized time and time again how closely tied my loyalty was to the standard societal beliefs of patriarchy, hyper-capitalism, and hustle. I began to understand, at a deeper level, how much these things contributed to my being anxious, exhausted, and burned out. I also realized more and more how tied my profession is to helping others at any cost – even to the helper's own well-being.

I heard a lot of, "I wish that I could go on a sabbatical," which filled me with shame. What made me think I was so "special" that I "deserved" to take time off like I was planning to do? And to take "purposeless" time off at that – I wasn't even taking a "traditional" sabbatical to study, write, or research something "important" and "meaningful."

This shame was a gut punch every time; it completely immobilized me–sending me into a shame shit cycle that would take me hours to come out of.

Then it hit me one day; I realized that most of the people who commented on how they wished they could go on sabbatical actually COULD if they truly wanted to. But instead, they simply decided NOT to.

Don't get me wrong; I totally understand the element of privilege that I have to have taken a sabbatical.

But also I worked hard to get to a place to be able to do so.

Yes, years of business growth and development.

But more so, months of work to specifically get the business to a place where I could step away.

Making financial decisions to save money so that my income was covered while I was gone.

The internal work of getting a better understanding of what wasn't working and what I was hoping to be different. (Getting clear on what should be different is something that is often overlooked, but if we aren't intentional about the new thing we're creating, we automatically go right back into the homeostasis of the old thing.)

Something like prioritizing my peace and joy over hustling toward another hire, expansion, greater caseloads, or higher revenue. Deciding when "enough is enough" is counter-cultural in this world of growth at all costs–of stepping away from perfecting and performing and people-pleasing.

So I finally started asking people, "Why do you think you CAN'T do it?" Which usually led to some uncomfortable silence (thankfully, as a therapist, I'm used to uncomfortable silence).

But sometimes, it led to some real discussion about what it would be like for them to step away from the grind, have space to get to know their heart's desires, and truly rest.

And those people started taking steps to plan their own sabbatical. And that was beautiful.

Standing on the Edge of a Cliff

"Come to the edge," he said.

"We can't; we're afraid!" they responded.

"Come to the edge," he said.

"We can't; We will fall!" they responded.

"Come to the edge," he said.

And so they came.

And he pushed them.

And they flew."

— Guillaume Apollinaire

I have a deep spiritual connection with cliffs. Especially when they are nestled next to a large body of water. The Napali Coast. Big Sur, California. Lima, Peru. Tulum, Mexico. Acadia National Park. Olympic National Park.

These are each amazing. But the one that has been the most life-changing for me has been my experience of the Cliffs of Moher – the iconic location in Ireland.

They're breathtaking. And terrifying.

There are no guard rails at the Cliffs of Moher—nothing to keep you from going over the edge. There's a little teeny sign right where the tourist area is, telling you to proceed at your own risk if you pass it. But that's it—no gate to keep you from crossing.

And did I mention the wind? Oh yes, the wind that whips up from the wild waves of the ocean and across the cliffs from every direction. There's a sense that it would whisk you away if it were to blow in the right direction.

The Cliffs of Moher feel overwhelmingly big. And dangerous. And completely captivating.

I had such a pull from the beauty and vastness that I couldn't help but take that initial step past the sign. With each step, I was drawn to take one more. And one more. And even one more. Farther than I could have ever imagined.

Yes, I was terrified (I am a rule-follower and fear-based Enneagram 6 Type). But I was also certain I did not fly halfway around the world, from Florida to Ireland, to regret not walking along the cliff.

Taking a sabbatical is like standing on the edge of a cliff. The wind is whipping. The waves are crashing below. You're dizzy from the height. You're even more dizzy from the beauty that pulls you closer and closer to the edge. You know full well what will happen if you go over the side of the mountain. But you have a distinct sense there's something beyond the initial drop. That, somehow, the wind that feels will lead to your destruction will also lead to your flight.

There's profound beauty and freedom in being willing to live in the land of the paradox. Exploring the both/and instead of living in the black and white.

To be clear, a part of you will die by going over the side of the cliff. There's the part of you that will fall away after that initial plunge. It will land in the wild, cold waters below.

You'll look down at the part of you that was ripped from your clenching fists. You'll wonder how you survived for so long by clinging to it. But, then, you'll look at the you that's left. And you'll feel free.

Then you will fly.

Let it Be

"Let it be" has been a mantra for me recently. If you're anything like me, the words bring to mind the classic Beatles song, and actually, the song is right on the money for the dual meaning behind the phrase.

The first meaning of "Let it be" is an acceptance of the present moment. It means bringing a sense of equanimity – a calmness and composure in all aspects of life, but especially to moments of challenge. It's a trust in life that things will ultimately work out. It's a resounding "YES!" to Albert Einstein's questions regarding the universe's friendliness.

"Let it be" is the space between pain and suffering. In life, there is pain. The hard things that happen, pain is the event. Often, the event of pain is unavoidable. Suffering, on the other hand, is our interpretation of the event. It's the story we tell ourselves about the pain. Suffering includes our thoughts, beliefs, and judgments about the situation.

Pain is unavoidable.

Suffering is optional.

Let it be. Here we are, on the edge of this cliff. Being here is uncomfortable. But I don't want to go back behind the sign because behind the sign is even more "uncomfortable." There's no fresh air to breathe there. The sky is not as brilliant.

The next step forward feels unattainable. But the suffering that you're afraid is coming is optional. Because what if it's everything you dreamed it would be??

And that's the other meaning of the phrase, "Let it be." May our dreams come to fruition. May we have greater peace, joy, and life in our lungs. May our dream be bigger than we could have ever imagined.

LET IT BE.

What's the Cost of NOT Doing It?

Oftentimes, when you're Stuck Between the World You Need to Release and the World You're Afraid to Enter, the cost analysis is incomplete. But, our brains are great about pointing out what could go wrong, the cost of doing the thing we're afraid to do.

But we're not as good at thinking about the cost of NOT doing the thing; of maintaining the status quo.

Why? Because inaction is action.

So the question is, where do you want to be in a year? In five years? Ten? What do you want your life to look like in twenty years?

How many hours of hustle, grind, and over-functioning will that be? What kind of toll will that take on your relationships? On your health? On your heart?

Take a moment to think about it…

No…*Really* think about it.

And, as a therapist, can I tell you a little secret?

I sit with people as they come face to face with the cost.

I've seen the hustle-harder culture consume marriages and relationships until they crumble. I've seen teens rail against parents who were never around. I've held space for retirees who lament the unfairness of the retired life they were forced to live, going from doctor to doctor to make up for years of not caring for themselves instead of going on the trips they always dreamed of. The hardest stories have been the grieving partners facing the reality of traveling alone.

Life isn't "supposed" to be that way. In a world where we implicitly sign a contract where we promise to hustle hard for our productive years for the payoff of peace and joy during retirement, there's a sense of betrayal that, more often than not, that doesn't happen.

But, for many, that realization comes too late.

For Such a Time as This

So the time to step into a Soul Sabbatical is sooner rather than later. To choose exquisite kindness over perfectionism, sufficiency and abundance over hyper-capitalism, gratitude and joy over scarcity, play and rest over hustle, and calm presence over chronic anxiety. Make choices now so that your future self can breathe.

We continue in the world that we need to release because we don't realize we have other options. So we do what we know, which is what we've seen all our lives. But then, at some point during our life's journey, we're grabbed by the shoulders, given a good shake, and shown that there is an option for another way.

If you're reading these words, this is your shake. It is not a coincidence.

If you're anything like me, you'll push back at that idea until you hear the message again somewhere else.

Then again. And again.

And, eventually, you won't be able to ignore it.

And you'll move closer to the edge.

And a little closer.

Then, you will fly.

The Courage and Love to Change

Realize this is a moment-to-moment journey. You've sown seeds of Faith, Hope, and Love. These seeds will grow when sprinkled with time, space, and intention.

It doesn't have to be done perfectly.

There is no perfect.

There's also no permanence.

You can't take a step that is so wrong that it will immortally damage you.

Not when the step is guided by kindness.

In one moment, the step forward, the tending to your soul, will be a whisper. At times it will be the roar of a lion. Sometimes the energy will be courage. Other times facing fear will mainly be from a place of love – for your current self, future self, and relationships.

Each moment brings you closer to your truth and the true you.

Without the hustle. Without the armor.

Allow your love for yourself to swallow you whole. To be lost in it.

Thank yourself for the patience you show to yourself.

Be the best listener of yourself that you've ever met.

Surprise yourself with how healthy you can feel– in your body, mind, soul, and spirit.

Fill yourself with the truth of who you are (really), not what you're not.

Support for Every Season

I love creating mantras for myself. I've found that having a statement that I can repeat to myself can help me stay out of old behavior patterns and remind me of the new way I'm practicing.

For example, when I find that I'm comparing myself to others, my mantra is:

Stay in your lane.

But, sometimes, Hustle Me is a bit more ornery and keeps trying to drag me back into the comparison shit show.

Then, the mantra becomes...

Stay in your m-f-ing lane, because boundaries with myself can be the hardest ones.

If I find perfectionism rearing its ugly head, I remind myself that...

Done is better than perfect.

When I find myself frazzled and trying to pack extra stuff into an already busy calendar, the order is to

Slow the fuck down.

When I'm feeling frazzled about a situation, I remind myself of my made-up acronym: AWO.

(Always Works Out.)

And these simple phrases help to bring me back to center.

What mantra are you practicing right now?

Words to Live By

I need all of the help I can get to counter my internal negative messages so that I can continue to put one foot in front of the other on this journey, to live from love, to remind myself of what I am over what I'm not, to identify that I need to give myself a bit of that.

My daily meditation includes a loving-kindness practice: a wish for happiness based on warmth, friendliness, goodwill, kindness, and love.

A traditional Loving-Kindness meditation includes internally repeating phrases like:

May I be safe.

May I be happy.

May I be healthy.

May I live with ease.

These are a great start, and over time I've found that discovering my own phrases that are meaningful to me and based on what I'm living at the moment are even more powerful – so that, moment by moment, I have love and courage to tap into.

To do this, I put my hand on my heart and settle into my breath.

Once my heart knows I'm listening, it can share its wisdom with me.

I ask my heart, "What do I need?"

And because the initial answer is usually, deceptively, my head answering, I ask again,

"What do I REALLY need?"

I know I've tapped into my heart when the answer I hear internally is something that, if it hasn't been fulfilled in a given day, my day feels a bit empty. These are universal needs of love, belonging, peace, health, strength, connection, or wisdom.

Then, I make note of the need. If the need feels a bit too far out of reach, then I wish myself to begin to take steps toward having the need filled (i.e., "May I love myself unconditionally" might start as "May I begin to love myself.")

Then, I ask my heart, "What do I need to hear?"

Are there any other Words of Affirmation Love Language people here? This is music to my heart!

Start by thinking of words you hear from others that are life-breathing.

"I love you."

"I'm here for you."

"I believe in you."

These are words that I'd love to have whispered into my ear every day of my life. Words that make me light up from the inside.

These can also be phrases that I'd like to remind myself that I know for sure, like "May I know I'm loved."

I make note of these and then take some creative license, led by the direction of my heart. I ask my heart to blend all of these into whatever I need for the moment.

It has looked a little like this...

May I know my worth.

May I trust my wisdom.

May I be a force to be reckoned with.

May I love and be loved.

And I offer this to you, until you create one for yourself...

May YOU know your worth.

May YOU trust your wisdom.

May YOU be a force to be reckoned with.

May YOU love and be loved.

Your Heart is Invited

Asking, "What do I need?"
Let's get clear about the difference between wants and needs:

Wants are personal and arise from the neck up. "I want a new car. I want a better job. I want the newest gadget."

Needs are universal and are discovered from your heart and body space. You hear the whisper in your heart and feel it in your guts. Universal human needs include safety, security, and belonging. They also include experiences of being known, cherished, seen, and heard. (PS. Being cherished is an innate human right. Do not question your being deserving of being cherished. If you're not being cherished, your life's mission is to start cherishing yourself, then find others to join you.)

A couple of notes about this practice:

Asking your heart, soul, and body what it needs might tap into unmet needs from your childhood. You might experience some sadness and grief from this fact. If this happens, be gentle with yourself. Take breaks as needed. Take some breaths or a walk. Place your hand on your heart and listen to music. Go to therapy.

If it feels like you have to rely on someone else to meet a need (a feeling of approval, for example), ask yourself how you would feel if you had that need met. Maybe having this particular need met would help you to feel safe, or give you a sense of value. Know that this sense of value, safety, peace, etc. can be your wish for yourself. These phrases that we're finding in this exercise should allow our hearts to finally rest.

Settle into a quiet space and connect with your heart. Breathe fully and gently.

Take a moment to be present to your heart and its wisdom. Let your heart know that you're listening and ask yourself:

"What do I need? What do I truly need?"

This should be a wish for yourself that, if this need is not met in a given day, the day does not feel complete.

This might sound like:

May I know that I am loved.

May I rest in my inherent value.
May I be kind to myself.

Now, close your eyes again and ask your heart a second question:

"What do I need to hear?"

Ask your heart what words it would like to hear, what words would bring the greatest delight, if your heart could hear them whispered in your ear every day for the rest of your life.

This might sound like:
You're a good person.
You're strong.
You are not alone.

You can use these phrases as is, or you can turn them into loving kindness phrases:
May I know my goodness.
May I feel my strength.
May I see how I am connected with others.

Find 3-4 phrases that resonate with your heart. Close your eyes and spend a few moments repeating them to yourself, making adjustments to the words and you hear feedback from your heart.

Then, repeat the phrases to yourself for several more moments, allowing them to settle into your heart. Once your heart is filled with the truth of them, notice how you feel. Gently release the phrases, knowing you can return to them at any time.

Chapter 7
Spiritual Practices- Prioritizing My Heart and Soul

Living a life of a Soul Sabbatical is, at its core, a spiritual practice.

For many of us, our relationship status with our hearts and souls and our spirituality would be "It's complicated."

When I meet with a client for the first time, one of the questions I ask is, "Are there any spiritual considerations you'd like for me to include in our time together?"

For most people, this question catches them off guard. How often are we asked to consider our spiritual lives, especially in how it relates to the other parts of us?

"Well, I don't go to church. I really should get back into it..."

I'm quick to point out that I'm not talking about religion or doctrine (although that's certainly a conversation we can have!), but rather how they connect with themselves with a sense of peace and purpose and how they interweave with their connectedness with the world that is bigger than them.

And in a world where we hardly carve out time to eat a meal that's not in front of a television or computer screen, we definitely don't take space for our spiritual world. But that's about to change.

As I shifted the energy of my day, I started prioritizing my morning routine. Instead of jumping out of bed and racing to an intense workout, I started lingering over a cup of coffee, meditation, and journaling. This invited prioritizing other things.

"Your body is really loving your spiritual practices."

I'm always curious about Tammy's feedback after a cranial-sacral massage (CSM), but this really caught my attention.

Soul Sabbatical

I met Tammy as we both worked at Combat Veteran Retreats – me as a trauma therapist using Accelerated Resolution Therapy and Tammy as the super popular massage therapist. I was seriously jealous every time a retreat participant would leave her treatment room and sing her praises.

So I had to see what it was all about. Because I treat trauma holistically (because The Body Keeps the Score and all), I knew CSM would be good for Veterans, the non-Veteran trauma survivors that I treat, and myself.

Tammy and I soon joined forces, and she will come and release additional trauma stored up in my trauma-intensive clients' bodies. I made it my routine to have my own massage to release any vicarious trauma that might build up in my body during an intensive, as well.

And when life started to feel like it was unraveling and I began to consider taking a sabbatical, I met with Tammy on a more regular basis to help me build a process to learn to tap into my body, wisdom, and intuition because I started noticing that as my body began to settle, I was learning how to trust myself and my needs even more.

Long story short, Tammy is pretty familiar with my nervous system. She's worked hard with me to help it unwind. A calmer nervous system leads to more connection – with ourselves and others. We're not living in a fight/flight/freeze/fix perpetual trauma response. We can access more joy.

Tammy is seeing my nervous system unravel up close.

"The calmer energy in your body reflects the spiritual practices you're shifting into."

Hmmm. This observation made me pause and consider what these practices are. These are things that have worked for me.

Explore these ideas, and others, for yourself and get curious about how your body responds:

- **Slow the fuck down** (I never would have dreamed that I would be writing about a spiritual practice that includes the word "fuck".)

Years ago, a friend shared that she was using this concept as her mantra for the year. I immediately let her know that I was stealing it and have used it liberally since, both personally, in my business, and in leading my team clinically.

The pace of life is so frantic that many of us don't know what it means to slow down. We know what it means to go full-force until we crash on the couch with Netflix, social media, and a bottle of wine.

We automatically fill any white space on our calendars. Seeing that I have thirty minutes unaccounted for means that I can fit one more errand, one more task, and five more emails into the day.

The imposter syndrome part of ourselves worries that if we slow down that everything that we've worked so hard to get will crumble and fall apart. The mask will crack, and people will realize we're not who they thought we were. Then, we'll recognize we're not who they thought we were.

But the illusion that not slowing down is safer moves us dangerously farther away from ourselves and our beautiful hearts.

Slowing down means that we might get a better understanding of ourselves, a better glimpse of our lives, and realize that not only are we not doing the thing we actually want to be doing, we aren't even the people we want to be. Only then can we make adjustments to anything.

- **Simplify**: Like "slow the fuck down," "simplify" often feels like two steps forward and one step back.

My friend, Erika, is a minimalist, and I'm slowly starting to understand the freedom that comes from this lifestyle. And while many of us consider our "things" when we think about simplifying, I'm finding much more calm in simplifying my calendar and relationships.

When Tammy was recounting our CSM history, she noted, "You used to go from this trip to that training to that other thing. Your pace would make my head spin!" (see also, slow the fuck down). But now I check in with the wisdom in my body when I plan things.

In fact, years ago, I took a business trip and managed to fracture my ankle as I stepped off of the airport shuttle to catch my flight. It was a random injury, and I was more embarrassed and annoyed about it then than I was concerned about it, so I hobbled around on a swollen ankle all of Memorial Day weekend before returning home. The minute my husband saw it, he insisted I go straight to the doctor. I was in a boot for ten weeks before it finally healed. I stayed too busy and had too many things on my calendar to follow up with the physical therapy that was recommended to me.

To this day, my ankle starts throbbing if I've got too much going on. The body keeps the score. When my body says slow down, I listen now. When I have a sense of dread about doing something, I investigate what that's about, and I stop trying to talk myself into doing something when my body keeps giving me a resounding "no."

The things that are exciting and energizing get space on the calendar. Things that are draining and feel like a chore are still there from time to time (I am a SLOW learner, and I still haven't found a way to make cleaning my toilets exciting, although that stays on my to-do list because I get immense value in having a clean toilet!), but each reminder that I don't find joy (or value) in doing them moves me closer and closer to releasing them.

This applies to relationships, as well. I'm tuning into how I feel when I spend time with people – those who energize and those who drain. I'm more aware of one-sided relationships (you know - the people who only talk to you when they want something) and distancing myself from them. I'm spending less time with people who only relate to me on a surface level and more time (much more time) with people who I connect with at a deep level.

In fact, several of these people don't live locally to me, and I prioritize traveling to meet them at a central location to spend time with them. Because there's less running around and doing other random stuff to contend with, this has become easier to do with more frequency. And I cherish every moment.

- **Meditation**: Meditation allows me to put "slow the fuck down" and "simplify" into practice on a daily basis.

I have been "practicing" meditation on and off for the past dozen years but I found a more consistent practice after finally finding a meditation app I truly enjoy using. As of this writing, I've logged more than 1300 consecutive days.

Given that, I believe each person has to find their right fit when creating a meditation habit, but it's nothing like the "empty your brain" notion that many of us think it is. For me, meditation has been much more of a self-compassion lesson.

I'm able to try to meet difficult emotions and experiences with kindness toward myself. Even when my brain is super busy, and it's hard to get any meditation going, I now just say to myself, "wow, look how busy your brain is today. That happens sometimes. It's ok."

Over the past several months, I've been practicing a Centering Prayer form of meditation, where I focus my attention on being in the loving presence of my Higher Power, Jesus. This has been life-breathing to my heart and is becoming a transformational process.

I've also joined a meditation group and have added a second twenty-minute sit to my day. I'm still building consistency with the second sit, but I almost find myself craving it. Given my history of trauma and chronic health conditions, my nervous system needs some extra TLC, and meditation is like hitting the reset button.

This means that on most days, I'm meditating a total of forty minutes. Yes, that's a lot of time, but otherwise, I would be pushing myself to work beyond what's healthy (or even productive), or I would be drooling on myself while scrolling mindlessly on social media.

It's taken years to build this practice. It started as a random five minutes here and there, but I'm so glad I stuck with it.

- **Journaling:** In 2018, my son Isaac gave me a journal and a set of colored pens for Christmas. I had never been a "journaler," but I had been researching the idea of bullet journaling to manage my time and energy across all the different "hats" I wear. I also needed a common space to keep all of my lists and projects organized.

I had no idea how to do this "bullet journal thing," but now that I had been gifted one, it was time to figure it out, so I tried out different concepts to get a feel for what worked for me. Over the years, my journals have grown from a place to keep track of my calendar, to-do lists, and notes about books I'm reading and courses I'm taking, to a place for me to explore who I am, who I'm becoming, the ways I'm getting in my own way, and how I'm growing as a person. The journals have become a creative outlet for me to dabble in artistically (I use that term loosely!!), as well as a scrapbook to document life and remind myself of what I'm grateful for.

Journaling has become part of my morning routine, along with my meditation and moving my body in some way. My journals helped me get through 2020 without losing my shit on people (for the most part), and I filled them up at record speed in the months leading up to and during my sabbatical as I was working through all my questions, fears, and ideas. Like many people, I had never been a regular journaler before building this practice. Like meditation, I had to play around with and explore the ways that resonated with me for it to work.

- **"Spiritual Gangster" Workouts and Playlist:**

My husband and I purchased a Peloton (along with many other pandemic buyers) during the COVID Pandemic. I had never taken a spin class before our bike being delivered, so I was hoping that I would enjoy the experience. I did enjoy it—a lot.

I also had never really worked out while listening to music, and soon discovered that I also enjoyed that. I think it's a big part of why I like the Peloton experience so much. As I explored the

Peloton platform, I discovered classes that are more emotionally and soul/spiritually focused than the heart-pounding workouts I had initially bought the bike for. I began to realize what a moving meditation these classes are for me. Oftentimes, the instructors would give me what became journal prompts. I started a playlist of inspirational and encouraging songs.

I started calling these classes my "Spiritual Ganger" classes (I don't know why. I think the words were on a workout shirt I bought). My very favorite version of the Spiritual Gangster Workout is to start on the bike, release the sweat, energy, and stuck emotions from my body, and then move to the yoga mat to look inward and consider some of the concepts and questions that were introduced on the bike. This way, I can check in with the wisdom of my body.

My Spiritual Gangster Playlist has grown to over 150 songs - not just ones that I've heard during class, but ones that I hear at church or that I come across while watching movies or TV shows that connect to my heart. I have it playing softly in the background as I journal and prioritize my days.

- **Yoga:**

Although I've mentioned yoga as part of my Spiritual Gangster Workout, it's important for me to discuss it from the lens of self-compassion, a concept that I like to think of as exquisite kindness and one that's core to our heart work.

I first tried yoga in 2009 as part of an assignment for a Spirituality in Social Work class I was taking in graduate school. I remember how much I struggled to force my body to get into the poses that the instructor I saw on the YouTube video so easily bent into. The more I struggled to force my body, the more rigid my body became.

I remember a moment of resignation when I took a deep breath and thought to myself, "I'm never going to be able to do this," and having my body soften just the slightest bit. I took another deep breath, gave my body permission to be where it was, and softened some more. The more I breathed and accepted where I was in the moment, the more I realized that yoga is just that.

I was also introduced to Dr. Brené Brown's research around the same time (and have since become a Daring Way Facilitator™), and through Brené Brown's work was introduced to Dr. Kristen Neff's research on self-compassion – the concept of giving yourself the same kindness and care that you'd give to a good friend.

For some reason, yoga and this concept of self-compassion clicked together in my head.

Like most of us, I have that Itty Bitty Shitty Committee, self-critical voice that can take up a lot of space in my head. But on the yoga mat, I can mindfully check in with where my body is at that movement, breathe, and be kind to myself. Instead of pushing into a pose, I think, "oh my, hamstrings. Look at how tight we are today! That makes so much sense after yesterday's hike! Thanks for all of your hard work. Let's just hang out here for a bit so you can feel better."

As silly as it sounds, it's slowly transferred to other parts of my life. I've taken what I've learned from my struggles on the mat and used the tool of exquisite kindness off of the mat. Now, when I'm struggling in my daily life, instead of criticizing myself, I say, "Oh, look at how scary this thing feels. That makes so much sense. I'm here with you, darling. You're not alone."

Restorative yoga, which looks a lot like a structured nap, helps me offer Hustle Me some compassion at the end of a long day. "Look at how much you got done; You can rest now. There are no more jobs to do." Restorative yoga is supremely helpful to calm the nervous system at the end of the day, can help to slow your brain down, and can ease your body into a restful evening.

The ending pose of Shavasana with each yoga class has been exceptionally helpful for me to practice moments of complete stillness in my day. This "corpse pose" is a way of integrating the physical practice of yoga, allowing it to be absorbed by the body. It's a moment of pause to thank yourself for showing up in whatever way your body, mind, and spirit presented in the class. Although this stillness at the end of class was difficult for me to be in when I first started practicing yoga, I've learned to appreciate it and even crave it. This is one more concept that began on the mat that I carry into other parts of my life.

- **CREATIVITY**: Creativity was a focus for me in 2022, and create was my word of the year (one of the reasons you're reading this book!).

During 2022, I would start each of my journal setups with a creative expression of this word, along with these definitions

- To bring something into existence
- The power to connect the seemingly unconnected.

This makes creativity a spiritual process – a reflection of my soul.

The things I create - whether it be a painting, something I've written, or a new therapeutic offering – are unique to me. So, although I'm not "artistic," and I've never necessarily considered myself to be a "writer" (until now!) – I've redefined "success" to be putting the creation into the world and allowing what comes of it (or not) to be what it is.

The thing I've created allows me to practice accepting what I have to offer with compassion and appreciation for what I've learned about myself along the way.

Creative outlets like puzzle making and cross stitch (glass blowing and stained glass classes are on my list) allow me to focus on things I find to be beautiful. Practicing creativity through improv classes that I've taken helps me to trust my intuition.

All things creative force me to challenge my perfectionism and help me practice beginner's mind, doing new things so that I don't fall into the rut of only doing things that I know I'm good at. This is totally uncomfortable every time I do it, but I've found that it gives me a firm foundation when things feel new and wobbly.

- **Nature:**

If anyone had told me ten years ago that I would be spending as much time in nature as I do now, I would have told them to take a hike (haha!), but now I'm camping, hiking, and paddle boarding regularly.

These were things that I've enjoyed doing for years, but they've taken on a new priority since the COVID-19 Pandemic. Now I'm much more intentional about putting these activities on the schedule. The intensity of life during COVID made me especially aware of how my body responds to being in nature. I realized how fully I breathe in the salt air of the beach and how my feet itch to be on a mountain trail.

Being in nature helps me to recharge, re-energize, refocus, and reprioritize. Nature brings me to the center of my wisdom. I take this process into the business and entrepreneurial side of life, too, and now I plan business retreats and Get Shit Done days around being in nature. As I write this, my partner and I are in Montana (a long drive across many states from Florida!) so that we can explore and balance work, play, and projects like writing this book.

- **Dreaming:**

Our hyper-productive, capitalistic culture pretty well brow beats any idea of life outside of the typical 40-80 hour work week and 6-8 figure salary out of the realm of possibility for most of us.

This changed for me when a business coach re-introduced the concept of dreaming and visioning my life outside of these constricting and suffocating norms.

Think about what it means to dream for a minute, outside of what happens for us during the night that we might or might not remember when we wake up.

A dream is a "cherished aspiration, ambition, or ideal." To dream is to "indulge in fantasies about something greatly desired."

When was the last time you marinated in a cherished aspiration? The last time you indulged in being in a heart space with something you greatly desired?

My guess is that you don't do it regularly. We get a taste of it and then shut that shit down because we're afraid; afraid it's not for us, we don't "deserve" it, or we're not capable of attaining it.

COVID-19 and the subsequent "Great Resignation" have shaken things up for many people, but if you sat down and wrote out how you would envision a "Perfect Typical Day," what would it look like? Beyond the typical five-year professional and financial goals, what would the best version of your life five years from now look like? Does your day-to-day life line up with the experiences you want to have, the trips you want to take, the people you most want to spend time with, and the body you want to live in?

While we might be stuck in a rut, what would it be like to create a new path to your future with anything being possible? Once we start with that curiosity, we realize that we have much more agency over our lives than we realize. The little changes begin to add up to something beautiful when we give ourselves permission to dream.

Letting Satisfied Be Enough – The Heart and Soul of an Ordinary Day

Today has been a soul-filling day. I have learned so many new things that my brain neurons are still pinging around, making new connections.

I have navigated the vulnerability of learning something new, not being an expert at it, making mistakes (and learning because that's how we learn), and being met with a chorus of "me too!" from my fellow learners.

I have given myself grace and compassion for every misstep, fumble, and not knowing. I have opened my arms wide with compassion for the part of me that was screaming, "What are you even doing here??!!" inside.

I celebrated the fact that I showed up.

I had deep, fulfilling conversations. For an introvert, those are the best kind.

I connected more with a community that, mere days ago, I did not know.

I walked away from this time filled, thankful, and exhausted. I literally took a short walk around my cul-de-sac to contemplate the time, get some sunlight, and move my body.

When I came back in, I knew that I had a commitment to myself to meditate and write. So I meditated on the beauty of smiles and laughter, of sharing difficult experiences and not being alone, and on my appreciation for the community.

And, at this moment, I'll let this satisfaction be enough. Without the goals or the metrics. Just now. Just here. My heart is full.

Your Heart is Invited

Settle into a quiet space. One where you can hear your heart without interruption.

Take several deep breaths. Place your hand on your heart. Feel your heart beating. Open to the warmth that is in your chest, just there under your hand.

Let your heart know that you're there and that you're listening, and that you're in no hurry.

Then ask it what it delights in. Allow a smile to come to your lips. And allow your heart's desires to flood the heart space. Meet your heart in these places doing these things.

Part Three
Hustle Check

Chapter 8
Addicted to Action: Spaciousness Rather Than Speed

W e are very busy people. In our culture, being busy means that we are very important. There are very important things that we must do. And we must do them very quickly and very well.

But, being very busy leaves very little room for margin and no room for spaciousness. Because we're addicted to the action, it feels very uncomfortable to be still. We literally experience Action Withdrawal.

So we stay busy until we crash—literally, crash.

We become one with the couch and whatever we're binging on Netflix, with another glass of wine or another bowl of ice cream, because we're also people who numb. We numb the uncomfortable Action Withdrawal. We numb the crushing busy.

I believe there's something else behind the numbing. I believe that the numbing, staying busy, social media scrolling, spending, eating, and all the others are the sleeping gas we use to lower the volume when our hearts tell us that things are not ok. Our hearts are trying to get our attention to say that, actually, things are too busy and too stressful, that this actual lived life is not how your heart desires to live. Our hearts are telling us this life is too rushed and lonely and that there are dreams that it wants to explore.

Your heart is trying to tell you that it's heartbroken. It doesn't usually scream, but if you keep ignoring it, it will get your attention through physical symptoms like stomach aches, chronic pain, and insomnia. Or maybe it will be through anxiety and depression. Through a general malaise, sense of discontent, and dis-ease that you can't shake, no matter how many shows you binge on, pills you take, or contracts you close.

Why? Because your heart wants to be heard.

Your heart is patient. It will wait for you to pay attention. But the intensity of its cries will increase and increase and increase. Like any good relationship, your heart needs time and space. Your heart wants to know it's important enough to make it on your busy agenda.

Let's explore the beatings of your heart...

The Year of Spaciousness

Several years ago, I started choosing a Word of the Year. Deciding on my Word of the Year is largely an intuitive process. I think about the year that's ending and the wins and challenges, strengths and opportunities for improvements, and think of what would have been beneficial for me to have had more of. I look at the year ahead, life events, and professional goals, then ask myself what I feel I need more of for the year.

2018 had been a doozy of a year. My schedule was booked with working Combat Veteran Retreats, helping our heroes heal from the effects of trauma, several trainings where I taught therapists cutting-edge trauma therapy techniques, doing deep trauma healing with clients, growing a business, and preparing and presenting on the TEDx UTampa stage. On the personal front, our family bought a house and moved, graduated our middle son from high school, and walked through my father-in-law's battle with ALS and that disease's increasing hold on his body.

Throw in the regular hodge-podge of meetings, appointments, travel, birthdays, and so on, and I knew something had to give and that I needed more spaciousness in my calendar and my day. As 2018 drew close, I recognized my need for margin and white space on my calendar and chose "Spacious" as my word for 2019. The word and the theme for the year took center stage in the vision board I created for 2019.

I'm amazed at how the word for the year unfolds each year. If you compare my calendar from 2018 – pre "Spacious" – to my calendar from 2019, you'd definitely see more space on 2019's calendar. But what isn't as tangible is the space that my heart needed. My father-in-law, Ron, passed away from ALS in May 2019, and it crushed the family and my heart more than I realized, as I was trying to be "strong" for my husband through the loss of his beloved hero.

Grief is a full-contact emotion, tackling you anytime and anywhere, usually without warning. As I continued to ride the waves of grief through the months after Ron's death, I realized how much my heart was swimming in the residual pain of the trauma work I do and grief around how dark humanity can be. In the deep trauma work that I do, it's not uncommon for me to hear stories that the grimmest movies are based on. And although it's part of my training to do this work in a way that does not negatively impact me, I realized that I needed to be even more intentional about the process of releasing this darkness.

To do this, I started to look for my own "intensive," my own "retreat," in order to do my own work. After a lot of searching and not finding exactly what I was looking for, I settled on a four-day minimally guided spiritual retreat at The Cove in North Carolina in November 2019. A big part of this choice was the beautiful location in the middle of the mountains and the fact that I could hike in between structured time there.

To be perfectly honest, my husband did not understand this. To be even more honest, neither did I. I didn't understand why I felt the need to do this so very intensely. Why did I have to be so "needy?" I don't like it when I do not understand things. Understanding things is what I "do." I wanted to just be able to wave some mythical magic wand and make the hole in my heart go away. I tried other things – weekend getaways and trainings, massages, girls nights out, date nights – but still, the calling lingered.

Shamon and I had many intense discussions about the time, energy, and money a trip like this would take. We both reluctantly agreed and we made a plan for the money piece; he would care of things at home, and I would address my need to go away. It was the first time I did something like this – where I didn't wrap a trip around work or try to fit it into another training where I could justify it as a "business trip." It was a trip that I needed for my broken heart.

And the spaciousness of the schedule, with extended time for prayer, meditation, and journaling, was a taste of what my heart needed. The space on the trail to have my mind go silent so that I could hear my own breath, the ritual of letting things fall away on the trail that needed to fall away, a placing of stones along the path to honor Ron, my clients, and my own heart gave me a feeling for what taking healing space could look like and feel like. It was four days of spacious healing, but not nearly enough. My heart was bandaged but still battered and bruised.

The four-day trip that felt like an eternity when I was planning felt like it was over in the blink of an eye. Still, a girl has to take what she can get, right?

Actually, this taste of what I needed planted the seed for what was to come.

The Year of Trust

Part of what was planted during my brief getaway was a seed of Trust. Trust in myself and trust that I could hear my own heart and take some action during a year that felt like the foundation was crumbling beneath our feet time and time again; I'm sure you can chuckle along with me at the irony that, for 2020 and all things COVID-19-related, my word of the year for 2020 was Trust.

Ironically, 2020 was the year that our church studied the Book of Job. If you're unfamiliar with the story, here's a brief recap:

Job is a stand-up guy—a follower of God. Long story short, he ends up losing everything – his kids, all of his possessions, his health. And through it, he trusts himself, and he trusts his God.

Time and time again, Job said something like, "I know my truth, and I know my God. It's going to be ok."

Time and time throughout the year 2020, I said something similar:

"I know my truth, and I know my God. It's going to be ok."

And more and more, I took space for my heart and space to be with God, building on some of the spiritual practices I learned during my retreat at the Cove.

I journal regularly and reread my journal at the end of the year to review the year closing and prepare for the next year. I was apprehensive about reading through my 2020 journal of reliving those difficult moments. Surprisingly, I found that the trust in myself and my God held. Time and time again. Was the trust there naturally, or because my WOTY had me focus on it? Both. But that's the point.

And that left me feeling...

She is Fierce

Fast-forward to 2021, when my Word of the Year was Fierce. The definition of fierce is "showing a heartfelt and powerful intensity." I was carrying spaciousness in one hand and trust in the other to see what Fierce in 2021 would look like. In many ways, it looked like holding fiercely onto the spaciousness that I was learning to carve out and holding even more fiercely onto trust – in God, in my people, in myself.

I could feel the shifts internally in my soul. After getting a taste of what having space to hear my heart, to dream, to feel, and to be, it became harder and harder to turn my back on myself. I met anything that tried to compromise those things with an unapologetic "no."

After testing the waters and knowing that I could, in fact, trust my heart and soul–despite years of people telling me that doing these things is untrustworthy, action based on faulty "flesh"-based emotions – I leaned into them more and more. And, every time, God was right there, holding me too.

So it was the combination of spacious trust and practice for the year of taking fierce action that began guiding me at that May retreat for the need to take a Soul Sabbatical.

What is a Soul Sabbatical?

When I first mentioned taking a sabbatical to my business coach, she was confused by my choice of words. In her mind, sabbatical is something religious leaders take. Others I have talked to have said they think of the world of academia when they hear the word. Sabbaticals might include travel, research, or writing.

I've found that it's important for everyone to be on the same page when it comes to words and what they mean, so let's dive into some definitions and how the phrase "Soul Sabbatical" came to be:

Sabbatical = "a period of paid leave" (to study), "of or appropriate to the Sabbath."

Hmm... That led me to the definition of Sabbath.

Sabbath = "a day of religious observance and abstinence from work", "to rest"

So resting is part of a sabbath/sabbatical, but what am I resting? My body? My mind? My SOUL? Oh, I was very soul-weary. To rest my soul sounded life-breathing.

Soul = "the spiritual or immaterial part of a human being," "emotional or intellectual energy," and "the essence or embodiment of a specified quality."

Hmm. I get a process of resting my body, and I can even understand resting my mind. But to rest in my spirit and my emotions? To understand those parts of myself more? Is that a thing?

So, a Soul Sabbatical means:

To rest in + study the spiritual part of your being, your emotional + intellectual energy, in order to better understand + love the essence + embodiment of your heart.

Yes, that sounded like something that would be helpful. The next step would be to craft what it would actually look like.

- What would you need to consider to be able to craft a soul sabbatical in your world?
- What parts of yourself are you curious about?
- What does one do on a sabbatical?

One of the top questions I got from people when I told them that I was taking a sabbatical was

Soul Sabbatical

What are you going to do?

I get it. Usually, when we hear about someone taking a sabbatical, they're traveling, studying a topic, writing a book, or something "big" like that. Also, we're pretty much a "doing" culture. Do you even exist if you're not "doing" something (and documenting it on social media)?

Whew! That felt like a lot of pressure. And it felt contrary to what it FELT that I needed — space.

So, aside from my hiking trip in Washington State on the front end of my sabbatical and an improv class that I took, my calendar was empty. (So empty, in fact, that I almost missed the first improv class because I was so much in my flow that I had forgotten about it. Thank goodness for Google Alert!) The hiking trip was an intentional physical distancing of myself from the business and clients and other things that I would too easily get pulled back into – for myself and the people around me, who I had conditioned to include me in everything (only to complain about this on the other side). I had the spaciousness of the trail, the Pacific Ocean, and a National Park with limited cell service. I chose to add the improv class to my schedule so I could spark my creative spirit and practice a paradox of both/and over yeah/but.

Instead of focusing on what I would DO during my sabbatical, I journaled about how I wanted to FEEL at the end of the sabbatical time. Feelings like ...

- "Breathed Up" (instead of feeling so weighed-down that it was hard to breathe)
- Spacious
- Energized
- Mentally stimulated in new ways
- Creative

- Peace
- At ease in my mind, body, and heart
- Excited
- Serenity
- Trust (held + secure in God and myself)
- Equanimity when faced with some of the hard things that come up when you open space for yourself in this way
- Playful
- Joyful

I made a list of activities I could choose from to help me feel this way...

- Meditation

- Exercise - spinning

- Journaling

- Hiking

- Yoga

- Video messaging friends

- Improv Class

- Cross stitching

- Reading

- Jigsaw Puzzles

- Cross stitching

- Lunch with my kids

- Glass Blowing

- Pottery making

- Being quiet with my thoughts

- Puttering around the house (can you tell I'm an introvert with these last two??)

Each day, I'd decide what I felt like doing. And I didn't do everything on the list. But thankfully, I don't have to be on an "official sabbatical" to check in with myself about what I need and do what I most need.

And I learned about myself by making these lists. There was a time, years ago, that I focused on adding "play" into my life, and that resulted in more paddleboarding, hiking, and other activities that I lose myself in.

As I prepared for my Sabbatical, I realized how much creativity I had been yearning for and how a lack of creative time led, in part, to my burnout. I noticed how energized I get when I do creative activities. So I added more of those things to my list.

This is the way that my Soul Sabbatical continues to this day, even though I'm back in the office.

My "Rules" for Sabbatical

Obviously, there are no true "rules" for what sabbatical looks like, but I knew that if I was going to take the time and energy to take a sabbatical, I needed to have some clear boundaries for myself about what was ok, what was not ok, and what "success" would look like:

The solution to overwhelm is nothingness. One premise about sabbatical is to allow yourself to move beyond the restlessness we face when we slow down and allow ourselves to experience boredom. The last thing I wanted to do was to clear my calendar of work, just to go on sabbatical and fill my days with different types of work, like catching up on housework, projects, and other busy work.

I took the way I wanted to feel as my job description for the sabbatical. Whenever I was tempted to do chores or busy work, I forced myself to pause and ask what I needed and wanted to do instead. As I've mentioned, because much of my burnout was from a lack of time and space for creativity, I added a list of new things I wanted to explore — like Improv!

I also had a couple of people I was talking with to help hold me accountable. I wasn't perfect, by far, but after the initial discomfort with stillness/boredom/not being "productive,/etc., I realized how good I was feeling, and that helped.

I found that, often, when people would talk to me about my Sabbatical, they would call it a vacation. Sabbatical isn't a vacation. Sabbatical is the work. While you're taking a break from your daily duties, you are focused on the work of listening to your heart and exploring its ways.

The sabbatical isn't the solution. It's not a magic wand you wave, never to feel depleted and weary again. The sabbatical is the space to guide you to the solution. Here's the deal... you might have a moment of great enlightenment and transformation during your sabbatical. As if the heavens parted and rays of sunlight beam down, and all of life is different, you suddenly have the solution to your heavy heart, your burnout, your weariness. A big sign that says "DO THIS NEXT!"

More than likely, however, your heart will speak to you more softly because that's how our hearts tend to speak. A bit here and a bit there. It will guide you to the next right thing. Then the next. And then the next. It will likely not present the next thing as a treasure map, where you can see the entire route and how X marks the spot.

Soul Sabbatical

Soul Sabbatical is an event, and it's also becoming my way of life. It will remain an ongoing practice for me in the remaining years of my life. The sabbatical is the journey.

Checking in with my heart to see what it needs sometimes leads me to a beautiful eleven-mile hike over one weekend with perfect weather. Other times, it leads me to curl up with my honey and enjoy our favorite show. Or be ok with being home on the weekend after a busy week, even as Hustle Me is scrolling the socials and screaming about FOMO. I can say no to Hustle Me more easily from the fierce space of the sabbatical.

"Self Care" is a hot topic these days. There's a whole industry built on selling you self-care, from the latest fad diet to getting your nails done, to whatever they're selling as the latest trend.

But what could change for you if you started viewing "self-care" as a way of living instead of a list of to-dos? What if you didn't have to rely on social media to tell you what to do to return to your true self, and you could trust your heart to guide you?

What if you tried out the diet, then checked to see how your body feels? Then continue with the diet if it resonates with your body and quit it when your body tells you that it hates being starved instead of abusing your heart by violating your body.

What if you got your nails done and were totally present for the experience, putting your phone down so that you could smell the lotion being used and see the face of the person touching you?

What if "Self Care" is being present in your life and noticing how your body and spirit respond?

Having a Mary Heart in a Martha World

There's a story in the Bible about two sisters that absolutely kicks my ass, as Bible stories do when I stop trying to study them with my head and read them with my heart. These two sisters, Mary and Martha, are Jesus' friends, and since Jesus had been busy doing Jesus things (like teaching and miracles and stuff), they thought it would be nice to invite him to the house for dinner.

Now, Martha is a top-notch hustler. She swept the floor, scrubbed the bathroom, and created the perfect dinner menu to celebrate teaching and miracles. No detail was too small for her keen eyes. The place was sparkling, the dinner was perfect, and the wine pairing was on point. She was proud of what she had done.

And Martha was resentful as hell. Because while she was busy with preparations for the evening, her sister dared to SIT AT JESUS' FEET. Just sitting there and doing nothing. Did she not see the cobwebs on the dining room light? Couldn't she just grab a dust cloth and take care of those things?

I might be taking some small liberties in the storytelling here, but this is definitely my interpretation because I can relate to Martha. And the Bible says that Martha was "distracted by all of the preparations," but I'm going to go out on a limb and say that not only was Martha resentful, but she also was EXHAUSTED (or maybe she was resentful *because* she was exhausted?? I've been there, too!)

And in all of my Martha-ness, I've thrown shade at Mary in the past. It must be nice just to sit around, chatting it up with Jesus. And Jesus even has the nerve to admonish Martha when she complains to him, telling her that her sister made the better choice. What the hell?

Because the telling of the story is centered around Martha, that's the character I always placed myself as. But one day, I was encouraged to read the story from Mary's point of view, as if I was her.

And my world turned on its axis.

As I put myself in the Mary role, I realized the peace she must have experienced during that visit. How she could actually enjoy and even remember it, instead of being so rattled and overwhelmed that she couldn't recall any detail other than the fact that the risotto was almost a disaster. How connected she was to herself and the other guests, and how present she was with Jesus, who was a hugely important person to her.

In fact, she was able to be present with Jesus and her immense love for him. And, more importantly, she was soaking in an experience of being loved simply for being present.

But, just like more than 2000 years ago, when this story was first told… simply being present isn't how our society operates. Choosing to put down the hustle, perfectionism, performance, and people-pleasing is as counter-cultural now as it was then. Probably more so.

But just like with these two sisters, when we choose this way, not only do we have space to experience more love, joy, and peace, but we help others realize that it is a viable option. And we can all build a little more courage to live counter-culturally.

There might be some resentment at first (did you know that the experience of resentment actually lives in the envy family – we have resentment because we long for something the person we resent has), but imagine being Mary, sitting in bliss, awe, wonderment, gratitude. And imagine carrying a Mary heart in a Martha world.

Wouldn't that be beautiful?

Your Heart is Invited

Make a Comfort Wisdom Layout. This is an opportunity to get as creative as you'd like, so pull out your journal, a sketch pad, markers, paints, and magazines to pull images out of. Create some space for this activity.

On the first page, list the things in your life that cause you to numb...

Work Stress

Relationship Stress

The Speed of Life with No Breaks

Boredom

On the next page, make a representation, with words or pictures, of what you use to numb...

Food

Exercise

Booze

Sex

Shopping

Doom Scrolling

Finally, allow yourself ample space to explore your Comfort Wisdom

Start with a list of ways that you would like to feel. What things and activities allow you to experience some of those feelings?

Nutritious Foods

Sleep

Movement

Soul Sabbatical

Music
Touch/Sex (the connecting kind)
Meditation
Yoga
Connection

Once you've gotten your representation of the things that bring you true comfort and a sense of spaciousness, take a picture of that list or page in your journal. Put a copy on your refrigerator or computer, or use it on the backdrop of your phone... any place that can remind you of your comfort wisdom options over numbing. Any place that can help you connect with your heart with spaciousness over speed.

Then choose one and do it.

Chapter 9
Integration: Bringing My Head and My Heart into Every Day

Integration

I spent the first month after returning from my sabbatical writing the word "Integration" across every calendar page in my planner and on every to-do list. I looked up quotes about integration and copied them into my journal, writing about them. With all of the time and effort that went into the planning and execution of the sabbatical, with all of the thought that I had put into its purpose and what I wanted to come from it, with as life-changing as it was, I didn't want to lose any pieces of it.

I wanted to bring all of the pieces into a unified whole. Otherwise, what was the point? I didn't want to look back and see the "things that I did on sabbatical" and regret that these weren't "the things that I did in real life."

And, although I was super-mindful and very intentional about the way I reentered the office with the amount of time I was there and the things that I did, I realized that the integration happens well before I step foot into work.

It was time for me to rethink long-held strategies for my day. Even more so, it was time to reconsider the energy behind every part of my day. It was time to reclaim energy from the hustle and reinvest it into my heart and soul.

Productive AF – Put Good Things Into the World (Head Check)

I am the queen of the To-Do list. I don't mean the "add tasks you've already finished to the list in order to mark them off"; I mean "keep adding stuff to the list, making it longer and longer, then crash and berate yourself for not getting it all done" to do.

Clearly, that doesn't work so well for me.

So I've tried playing around with different versions of the To-Do List. Some options that maybe aren't so, shall we say, "militant"?

I started by calling my list Easeful Productivity, with an emphasis on the "easeful," but the energy of "productivity" was still there. And, basically, productivity trumped easeful. Old habits die hard and words are powerful, so it was time to explore other words.

As I began cultivating a spirit of creativity in my life, I tried adding that word to the mix. Easeful Creative Productivity. That has a nice ring to it.

But no. Still a no-go. That pesky productivity really has its hook in me.

I finally realized that "productivity" calls forward Hustle Me. Ironically, Hustle Me is counterproductive to the space, time, and flow that creativity needs. Let me say that again – creativity, the things that I bring into the world that are unique to me, the ones that only I can offer, needs time and space to be breathed into existence. If I don't prioritize that space, my legacy is simply repeating what already is. When people talk about me when I'm gone, I want them to say more than "she was awfully productive."

I also realized that I'm already "productive" in the most important areas, without needing a list to remind me of what needs to get done. The list is a taskmaster that I don't actually need to get those things done.

So I did something that felt big and scary — I got rid of "productivity." And because I want to ensure that creativity doesn't turn into the next thing to be "productive" with, I held on to the word easeful. Not that creativity is EASY, but it also can't be, well, militant. Militant energy kills all things creative.

Now, a "good" day is measured by the shit I got done but also by the space I've given myself to be creative. In fact, the creative process energizes me so that I CAN do other things, so I prioritize creative space first thing in my day. And I don't have to sacrifice one for the other.

What's a "good" day for you?

I'm absolutely not anti-productivity. I believe that part of our calling is to identify the thing we were uniquely placed on this planet to do and do that thing.

What I'm saying is let's stop trying to do our thing, as well as everyone else's thing, and all the things. This is exhausting and robs us of the best parts of ourselves to bring forward into the things we're passionate about.

When we stay in our own lane, in our calling, and operate from our heart center, as well as our head center, we can find a flow and ease to put forth something of excellence. And we're productive AF and energized.

Seasons of Hustle? (You Better Check Yourself Before You Wreck Yourself!)

I was talking to my hairdresser recently. When you spend hours sitting in a chair that goes up and down and around in circles, with your hair sticking out in all directions, you tend to have lengthy, in-depth conversations with the person on the other end of the pair of scissors. (P.S. If you regularly find yourself falling asleep during your hair appointments because you're not used to sitting still for that long, you could likely benefit from slowing down more often!)

Victoria was with me during the whole sabbatical process, and we've talked together quite a bit about our society's hustle, along with the beauty of slowing down. Victoria is in a different season of life. I'm a middle-aged empty-nester, established in a career and an expert in my industry.

Victoria is young, in the early stages of her career, with a new marriage and a young child at home. She's full of energy and drive, with big professional aspirations that have her traveling for specialized training so that she can make a name for herself and master her craft.

I can relate a lot to Victoria.

Victoria caught me a bit off guard when she asked if I thought that it was "ok" to have "seasons of hustle."

What a fantastic question! And I totally didn't have an answer for her... at first.

So I took a breath and thought for a while about what it's like to be Victoria. I did some perspective-taking about her situation and thought back to when I was in a similar stage. I thought about the wisdom that has come over the years (mostly hard-fought and painful learnings and what I wish my younger self knew back then).

I also really honed in on something that Victoria said when she shared about her recent training trip. I noticed that she mentioned how she was intentional about not packing her already-filled, long training days with additional tasks.

It also struck me that she planned her travel and work schedule to have a down day between returning home and returning to work with long days of seeing clients.

And I realized that, by definition, what she was describing was NOT hustle! In fact, Dictionary.com defines "hustle" as:

Soul Sabbatical

To force (someone) to move unceremoniously in a
specified direction
To obtain by forceful action or persuasion
To coerce or pressure someone into doing or choosing
something.

I don't know about you, but each of those definitions feels
slimy. I wouldn't hustle someone else. Why would I want to
hustle myself?

Well, because it's so alluring. Hustle feels like the answer. It's
what we're taught. It's what we know. We think we can do it
and not suffer the consequences. We think it's "just this once."

But we're so wrong, because it turns out that this hustle is
addicting and is positively reinforced by our culture.

Still, what are we supposed to do during particularly busy
seasons of life? How do we move forward with professional
goals without falling into hustle mode?

I like to think of it more as "seasons of acceleration." The pace
of life and responsibilities and expectations of our time and
energy are greater during these seasons than they usually are,
but they're sustainable for a specified period of time. And we're
regularly checking in with ourselves (honestly!) about how the
pace feels.

Think of hopping in an Uber to get to your desired destination.
If your driver guns the engine and the tires squeal at a break-
neck pace, you are not likely to rate them very highly or leave a
big tip. In fact, you might report them as an unsafe driver.

But if your driver flows smoothly with traffic and you find yourself
at your destination without whiplash from their forceful action of
driving and braking hard... now we're talking! And if your driver

navigates the roads in such a smooth way that you actually find yourself enjoying and even energized by the journey, now that's a trip you'll take the time to leave a raving positive review about!

When considering putting this into practice, keep this GPS metaphor in mind. Are you coming up on a busy season in your life, perhaps completing a challenging certification or a big project at work? Maybe there are many things going on in your personal life – a vacation or back-to-school time for your kids. Maybe there's a series of medical appointments, a move, or life changes like empty-nesting, marriage, divorce, or the death of a loved one.

Whatever it is, start with a realistic overview of the journey. Put every single appointment and commitment on the calendar. Block out your schedule with appointment times. Seeing this can often be a sobering reminder of our time-space continuum constraints. There are only so many hours in a day. We have limited energy (no matter how many energy drinks or cups of coffee you try to slam).

Consider your different GPS route options. The "most direct route" might not be the most "fuel efficient." For example, when I was completing my undergraduate degree, my children were very young, and my husband was both attending school and had a demanding full-time job where he traveled often. I have chronic health conditions that were not well managed at the time, so I faced significant fatigue challenges. Because I had stayed at home before returning to school, I knew such a big change would significantly impact the family (not to mention a huge adjustment for me), so I decided on the "scenic route" while I completed classes part-time.

By the time I was considering my graduate school options, the kids were older and could help out more. Everyone was more accustomed to a new routine, and I was ready to take the "express route" to complete an Advanced Standing program in a year.

Living a Soul Sabbatical means that you're intentional when entering seasons of acceleration. You weigh the pros and cons about doing so (when you can. Sometimes life slingshots you into such seasons.) You stay in tune with your heart and your body. You default to rest mode when you need it, even (especially) if there are still things to do. You prioritize sleep, nutrition, and moving your body.

YOU DON'T USE WORK TO NUMB THE HARD EMOTIONS. (Read that again.) They're still there and won't go away just because you're ignoring them. You know this. Stop thinking this time will be different. And remind yourself of this regularly when you find your hours at work slowly creeping up... again.

I'm learning to bookend travel with a rest day, especially as post-COVID travel seems to be more and more challenging. I have a yoga mat and meditation cushion tucked away at the office, and travel with my yoga mat. I carry my water bottle everywhere I go. I don't "work through" lunch. I nourish my body with real food, away from screens.

I'm more discerning about what I say "yes" to. In fact, as I'm more and more honest with myself about what's most important, I'm saying "no" to more and more things. My brain and body don't do well with sitting for hours on end, so I limit the work that requires me to do so. When I structure therapy sessions, intensives, workshops, retreats, or other work offerings, I either include movement in the structure or long breaks that allow for it.

Sometimes I need to re-calculate my route because things take longer to do in a healthy way (I'm notorious for expecting things to be done more quickly than is realistic). There are gas stations (rest, yoga, creativity, connection) for me to refuel at along the way. I am not a machine. Neither are you. It's time to stop treating ourselves as if we are.

So, have the goals and ambition, and drive. Do the big things. And enjoy the journey without sacrificing your soul.

Delighting in Pleasure

When was the last time that you paused to savor a moment? Is it something that you allow yourself to do? Or do you press on to the next goal, task, or item on your to-do list?

Because we're addicted to action, we tend not to slow down, much less pause. Because we run on anxiety and remorse, our thoughts jettison to the future or linger in the past. Because we're so disconnected from ourselves, we rarely notice simple delight. Because of our brain's negative bias, we tend to focus more on the things that are wrong or that we don't want. Because of our scarcity mindset, what we actually have is never quite enough.

I've discovered that living a life of a Soul Sabbatical means that I intentionally look to delight in pleasure. I seek out joy. Not in a hedonistic way, but in paying attention to what's right in front of me.

These are regular, daily experiences, like the taste of chocolate or my favorite meal. The warmth of the dogs lying across my legs. The hug from that person who gives the best, full-body hugs. The sound of laughter during our team's "social hour." The comfort of my "special blankie." Heated seats in the car (even during Florida summers). The stunning colors of the sunset against the backdrop of the lake just down the road from my house blows me away every single time that I turn the corner of the road.

These things are here for you, too. They beg to be experienced. You can start now.

The definition of "savor" is "to enjoy or appreciate (something pleasant) completely, especially by dwelling on it."

I think that there are three things that keep us from being able to savor our lives:

1. We don't pay attention to the pleasant things that are right in front of us. We think that pleasure, joy, and gratitude have to be about the "big" things, so we miss the everyday beauty, usually because we're moving too fast and not in tune with our heart's response.

2. "Completely." Most of us experience things by thinking about the experience. Because our society places so much emphasis on cognitive "knowing," we miss out on knowing things completely... not only in our minds but in our hearts and bodies, as well. In short, if you only think about the thing you're savoring instead of actually *feeling* it, you're missing out on the best parts. I'm a brain geek (as a trauma therapist), and the memories (positive or negative) that stay with us the longest are the ones that are embedded in our bodies and senses – the sounds of delighted squeals, the taste of your favorite holiday dish, the smell of a loved one's cologne, the feeling of warmth in your chest from a hug. What does "delight" feel like in your body? Where do you feel peace? Joy? Excitement? Contentment? If you're not quite sure, think of a time that you would describe as delightful, joyful, or peaceful. Recreate the whole scene in your mind. Where were you? What did you hear, see, smell, taste? Now check in with your body below your neck. What sensations are you feeling in your body?

3. "Dwelling." Again, because we're Addicted to Action, we tend not to dwell. We shop Instacart to avoid lines at the grocery store, roll through stop signs, and get annoyed with the time it takes to brew a cup of coffee or steep a cup of tea. (There was a great scene recently on the popular TV show, The Crown, where the instruction was given that tea is not to be gulped but cherished through sips. How rich our lives would be if we adhered to that!) We think "dwelling" is for people who don't have busy, productive lives. Guess what? You don't have to be old and retired, with nothing else to do, to "dwell"!

Or, what if... maybe dwelling is for people who want to nourish their souls and experience delight, joy, and peace. The more we linger in those moments, the deeper they seep into our spirit. The more easily we can return to them in the future when we can use a little dose of delight during a difficult day.

To be clear, all moments are temporary, whether positive or negative. And I'm not talking about "toxic positivity" and saying that this process "fixes" all the hard things we face in life. But when we tune our eyes to recognize pleasure, we find it's more abundant than we realized, so we don't have to worry that there's a limited supply. When we redirect our negative frame of mind to find the tiniest positive, we can find a bit of expansiveness instead of constriction.

Interestingly, these moments of joy can feel super vulnerable. If I open my heart to the bliss of my loved one's head resting on my shoulder, my brain can jump to impending doom – "Holy shit. Things are too good right now. Clearly, something bad is about to happen." Even these moments, when met with explicit gratitude for what is true at this moment, can help us to know that these moments of joy will always be present – even when something bad happens.

Before you know it, you might find that you're following this feeling of expansiveness and including more life-breathing things in your day that feel that way and fewer things that don't. Refuse to deprive yourself of the tiny, splurge-y pleasures that spark joy in your days. This is the key to the Soul Sabbatical.

Your Heart is Invited

We've explored the headspace. We've explored the heart space. We've introduced the two to one another. Now, let's explore how to integrate the two more regularly.

A Soul Sabbatical is about owning your desires in addition to your responsibilities. It's about learning to listen to your deep wisdom to guide your days.

For me, this looks like journaling daily. I start with the same prompts:

I'm thankful for:

I'm trusting God for:

I'm joyful about:

My heart is...

Easeful Creativity:

You don't have to have a formal journaling practice to check in with yourself about how your head and your heart will guide you through the day but identify 2-3 questions you can ask yourself each day.

They might include...

Conclusion

Conclusion

Deeper Still

My husband and I returned last week from a month of working remotely from Montana. We first visited Glacier National Park two years ago, and if it weren't for that, I wouldn't be able to tell you where on a map Montana is located. I remember leaving the airport on our way to our hotel and passing a billboard that said, "Montana, where you come to visit and decide to stay."

Hmm... you're a little full of yourself, aren't you, Montana?

But Montana wasn't. I fell head over heels in love and wanted to go back before we ever left. We immediately started talking about how, when we returned, we wanted to spend an extended period of time to explore more of the state's rugged beauty.

So, several months ago, when we put money down on an Airbnb, it was the fruition of a two-year dream. And as the time got closer and closer for us to actually drive four days across the country and be away that far physically for the first time, I started to panic. For several reasons, it wasn't a good time to be "away" from the business.

I found myself wanting to slide into hustle mode, as I am prone to do. I started to scramble to find ways to add more paying work to my calendar while we were gone. We thought about canceling the trip.

Then I thought, "what if this is exactly what is meant to happen? What if it's exactly what we need?"

We packed up the truck and drove four days across the country – from Florida and across twelve states.

And with each mile, I felt a little more of the worry, a little more of the heaviness, fall away. And I started getting some clarity about what Montana was actually for... writing this book.

Conclusion

And hiking. We hiked 100 miles during our month away. And it was glorious. There's no such thing as a bad hike in Montana. And it was challenging.

And I was able to write. Being in nature with my feet on a trail is a moving meditation for me. My brain was connecting stories and thoughts, and when we returned to the Airbnb, the words flowed onto the page.

I never thought of myself as a writer until now. I never expected to write a book, but as I've shared parts of my experience and heard others' stories, I've realized there is some commonality in what we live, so I've been putting thoughts onto paper. I expected it to be challenging, and sometimes it was. More often, though, being in such expansive spaciousness allowed a flow.

Now, we're back home, and although reentry is always a bit rattling for me (especially as an introvert going from a town of 5000 in Montana to a major metropolis of nearly three million people in Tampa Bay), I'm noticing a shift.

Everything that I've been writing about, I'm feeling at a slightly deeper level. I'm slightly better about slowing down slightly more and allowing time and space for my journal. I'm slightly more trusting of what's happening, recognizing the things I can't control, and leaning into more serenity under duress and equanimity for these things.

It's like recognizing that I can allow the chair I'm sitting in to hold me 5% more than I realized it could hold me before. I've come a long way on my Soul Sabbatical journey. And, also, 5% more feels really good.

I'm sure that, at some point in the future, there will be another 5%, or 3%, or 20% – because I don't believe I will ever have "arrived" at some magical point where there's no opportunity for growth.

Conclusion

I'm here, holding space for my next 5%. I'm here, holding space for yours, too.

Like Montana, your heart has been waiting for you to come to visit and decide to stay.

Will you answer the call?

A Love Letter to Gen Z

A Love letter to Gen z

A Love Letter to Gen Z

Dear Weary Gen Z'er,

We tend to share stories from our own perspectives. That's the way story-telling goes, right? When I first wrote my letter to Hustle You, I wrote it to that part of myself. The part that had been hustling for nearly 50 years.

I had no idea how much it would resonate with you and your weary heart.

But I started hearing how it resonated for you. That you found yourself tearing up, but you didn't quite know why.

And I get it.

Every generation that has come before you has struggled with the Hustle Culture. But yours is different.

You had the Millennials who challenged things in a way that hadn't happened before to lay a foundation for you. Your growing-up years were book-ended by planes crashing into buildings and a global pandemic. You worked your ass off in AP, IB, Dual Enrollment, and the other academic classes you were told you had to have to be successful. You added all of the extra-curricular activities and volunteer hours required for you to be considered for the college you wanted to attend. You accumulated a ton of debt to get the degree that would guarantee that you'd make six figures upon graduation. Then you couldn't actually get hired.

When you finally landed a job, it was making much less than you thought you'd be making, and far less than you actually need to pay back student loan debt and account for inflation.

And you hate your job.

The cards have been stacked against you. You were burnt out before you even got started.

A Love Letter to Gen Z

And this practice of Soul Sabbatical? This is for you, too.

Your heart is crying for your attention. And since you're a bit more in tune with it, maybe you can teach the people around you a bit about how to listen.

Much love,

Your Soul Sabbatical Guide

Gratitudes

From the depths of my heart...

Shamon, for the most pure love I'll ever know. Thank you for taking this journey with me, for choosing me time and time again, and for believing in me always.

To Christian, Isaac, and Abby:

The best feeling in the world is when your kids are proud of you. Thank you for growing me into the person I am today and for your love and support.

To Mom and Dad:

Thank you for always loving me in the very best way you've known how. I love and appreciate you.

To Kelly Higdon:

For teaching me to dream again and for seeing in me something bigger than I could see in myself. Thank you for helping to hold space to make the sabbatical happen.

To Dr. Brené Brown, Dr. Kristen Neff, Terry Real, LICSW, Father Richard Rohr:

My professional and spiritual mentors. Your work has shaped me and is woven into the heart of this book. Thank you for stepping into your gifts and, although you don't know me, guiding me to step into mine.

To Ally Love, Christine D'Ercole, and Denis Morton:

For Sundays with Love, Reflection, and Reset rides (and yoga!). For your words, for the music, for the laughter, cursing, sweat, and tears. For the challenge in my body, as well as in my mind and heart, to slow down or to push (How is it that EVERY time I think "Reset" means, "Come close and let me whisper sweet nothings in your ear", but in reality it's "Let's strip away the mud to uncover the Golden Buddha within.) Thank you for reconnecting me with my body and heart and for being such a vital part of this journey. Your classes are my therapy.

To Jo Muirhead and Adam Davis:

Thank you for gently nudging me and for showing me how my words impacted you, which gave me courage to keep putting them on the page. These would still be journal entries if it weren't for you.

To Tori Calandro:

Thank you for sharing how my words impacted you with your amazingly beautiful illustrations. Cheers to our first publication!

To Erika Labuzan-Lopez and Becca Williams:

My world is a much less lonely place knowing that you're a Polo away. "Thank you" does not encompass everything you mean to me, so let's have a margarita and a hike together. But probably not at the same time.

To Rebekah Varney:

To one of the most beautiful souls that God has created. Thank you for your love, your support, your obedience, and your courage. It's contagious.

To all of you who cheered me on in this process, in big and small ways, thank you for your love and support.

About the Illustrator
Tori Calandro

From as young as she could remember, Tori always held a sketchbook by her side. It began as a simple collection of drawings, she would practice the cartoons seen on TV or the books read in school. Dreaming throughout her childhood to one day become an illustrator. Grabbing out her sketchbook as soon as she got home from school and created her own comic books, visual stories, or pieces of work that held space on their own. And as she grew, so did the expression in her drawings. Her sketchbook became an evolution from holding light-hearted drawings to a sanctuary of her emotions. It became a silent confidant, a place she could go knowing she could trust it to hold her deepest thoughts and emotions, and ultimately became the truest reflection of her feelings.

Embarking on her academic career, Tori attended the University of South Florida majoring in Integrative Public Relations and

Advertising, and earned two certifications, Marketing Sales and Visualization and Design. Both certifications taught her how to develop the world of visual storytelling where she learned many skills to adapt thoughts into a visual representation.

Never had she thought her childhood dream could become a reality, but fate has a funny way of coming full circle. And so, a few years after graduating college fate came knocking in the form of Yolanda. Providing her a chance to not only create visuals to match Yolanda's beautiful writing but to embrace the part of her who knew all along that she could be— an artist. And with every illustration Tori found herself evolving not just with her craft but within herself.

So, as you turn the pages of Yolanda's book and journey, the illustrations represent more to me than just ink on a page — they are the manifestation of a lifelong passion coming to fruition and a tribute to the power of believing in yourself.

Note to the author

Yolanda:

Illustrating for a book that holds so much vulnerability, strength, and resilience in its pages has been an honor of a lifetime. Thank you for trusting me to be a part of your journey and for allowing the little girl in me to now know that I wasn't dreaming too big. This book will change many lives and I know for me it already has in more ways than one.

And I can't wait for the world to read it.

Tori Calandro

About the Author
Yolanda Harper, LCSW

While many authors know all of their lives that they want to become published, Yolanda Harper's first book, Soul Sabbatical, started as a series of journal entries written during a burnout "meltdown" that led to her taking a sabbatical from her roles as a trauma and relationship therapist, researcher, trainer, mental health thought leader, and business owner/entrepreneur. As she shared more about her experience, she realized how much people resonate with the idea of a sabbatical, but don't know how to step back from the demands of hustle culture to take one.

Using her understanding of trauma, neurobiology, and the broken systems we live in, Yolanda wraps words around our lived experiences. As if you're sitting down with her and a cup of coffee, she says the things that you're thinking in your head, helps you to understand that you're not alone, and walks you through ways to reclaim your time, energy, and joy.

Yolanda is a warm-hearted music and nature lover who has a strong faith and likes #TrailLife. She is real; a therapist, mental health thought leader, entrepreneur, TEDx Speaker, Soul Sabbatical Doula, wife, and Mama always to her grown children – but a human first.

She is brave – not afraid to tackle the grit, whether on the hiking trail or in life. She leads with humanness and enjoys authentic connection with others, bearing witness to their world of tears, laughter… the whole shebang. She invites you to come home to your heart.

Printed in the USA
CPSIA information can be obtained
at www.ICGtesting.com
LVHW010730171023
761309LV00005B/491